AT THE FEET OF JESUS

BY
PAM JENKINS

Cover Design by:
Denise McBrayer

Trafford Publishing Company
CANADA

Note for Librarians: A cataloguing record for this book is available from Library and Archives
Canada at www.collectionscanada.ca/amicus/index-e.html
ISBN 1-4120-7710-9

"Scripture quotations taken from the New American Standard
Bible®, Copyright ©
1960,1962,1963,1968,1971,1972,1973,1975,1977,1995 by The
Lockman Foundation. Used by permission." (www.Lockman.org)
Scripture quotations identified KJV are from the King James
Version.

To order additional copies of this resource: Write
W.O.W. International, Inc.
P.O. Box 849
McDonough, GA 30253
Phone: (678) 232-5830

*Printed in Victoria, BC, Canada. Printed on paper with minimum 30% recycled fibre. Trafford's print shop
runs on "green energy" from solar, wind and other environmentally-friendly power sources.*

TRAFFORD
PUBLISHING™
Offices in Canada, USA, Ireland and UK
This book was published *on-demand* in cooperation with Trafford Publishing. On-demand
publishing is a unique process and service of making a book available for retail sale to the
public taking advantage of on-demand manufacturing and Internet marketing. On-demand
publishing includes promotions, retail sales, manufacturing, order fulfilment, accounting and
collecting royalties on behalf of the author.

Book sales for North America and international:
Trafford Publishing, 6E–2333 Government St.,
Victoria, BC v8t 4p4 CANADA
phone 250 383 6864 (toll-free 1 888 232 4444)
fax 250 383 6804; email to orders@trafford.com
Book sales in Europe:
Trafford Publishing (uk) Limited, 9 Park End Street, 2nd Floor
Oxford, UK ox1 1hh UNITED KINGDOM
phone 44 (0)1865 722 113 (local rate 0845 230 9601)
facsimile 44 (0)1865 722 868; info.uk@trafford.com
Order online at:
trafford.com/05-2606
10 9 8 7 6 5 4 3 2

Dedication:

To my Lord and Savior, Jesus Christ, Who is worthy of all honor and of all praise. I lay this at your feet my sweet Savior, for You alone are worthy. Draw your daughters to Thy feet that their hungry soul may be fed, set the captive free, pour forth the fountain of forgiveness upon the sin sick soul, bind up the broken hearted, help the lost find their way home and let the works of Thy hands praise thee forever more.

Foreword

I am eternally grateful to many people for this book of which I would like to name a few. For Steve, my husband and best friend, thank you for sharing your wife, for sacrificing so much so she can do what God has called her to do, I love you. For Steph and Kris, who unselfishly love their mother in spite of her many flaws. You make my heart sing. I love you and am so proud of the young women you've become. For my mother, who prayed for a wayward daughter until she found her way home. Thank you for believing in me. For Pastor Buddy Norton, thank you for leading me to Jesus. Your labor of love has not been in vain! For my Aaron and Hur, thank you for holding up the hands of this lowly writer. You are beautiful to me, I love you my precious friends. For my sweet friend Vickie Nation, who has encouraged me immensely. Thank you for being who you are to me. And for Pastor Tony Stinson, for his invaluable wisdom and guidance to this beginner writer who had no clue. Thank you for wise counsel.

God's callings can take us by surprise. Have you ever felt overwhelmed by the calling of God on your life? A calling so great that you felt you could never attain it? For several years God has stirred my heart to write. Not knowing what to write or how to write, I did the only thing I knew to do, I fell at His feet in full surrender and in total desperation. It was there in those moments spent at His feet that, *"At The Feet of Jesus"* was birthed. It is His calling, and it is His book. It has changed my life. I do not consider myself a writer, but only the hand that God has chosen to be His instrument. For you, precious student, who have chosen to pick this book up and open its pages, I am humbled and so very grateful for you. I pray that your life will be blessed. You hold in your hand what is untold hours spent seeking Him and surrendering to His will, penning every word as He spoke it to my heart.

As you journey through these pages, you will find seven lessons containing four days of study. So for each lesson, you will have four days of study time allotted. Each lesson will have a memory verse so the Word of God will be stored in the treasury of your heart forever. I have, for the most part, used the New American Standard for our scripture references, as I believe it does not compromise the Holy Scriptures. Besides your bible, you will need either some highlighters or colored pencils. You will need a quiet place to take this study. A place where you can sit at His feet. The format for each week is simple beloved and easy to follow. Each lesson will begin with prayer and then guide you through the scriptures using observation methods, probing questions and word studies that will help us see truth and the benefits of those truths. I believe every Bible Study is different for every person who takes it. Bible studies are personal journeys for each of us who give ourselves to them. Though I may never see you face to face, I have prayed for you beloved student.

Acts 20:24 states: "But I do not consider my life of any account as dear to myself, in order that I may finish my course, and the ministry which I received from the Lord Jesus, to testify solemnly of the gospel of the grace of God."

This is why I have written this book. May your life be forever changed as you dwell at the Master's feet.

Table of Contents

"At the Feet of Jesus"

By: Pam Jenkins

Preface

The star had shown brightly overhead illuminating the
darkened sky showing them the way in which they must
go. This journey would take them across the dessert
sands, over the rugged terrain of the distant mountains
and beyond the great waters of the deep. So brilliant was
its light and captivating was its appearance that they
cared not what lay ahead, only that they follow until they
find the promised one. The child born unto them, God
Himself, wrapped in swaddling clothes lying in a manger.
They knew this star would show them the way to this
child, this child whom they longed for ages past to bow
and worship. These wise men had but one desire, one
destiny; to sit at the feet of their King, their deliverer, the
one who would be called Emanuel, God with us. Why did
these men forsake all just to bow at the feet of Jesus?

They knew that some day the feet of this tiny baby would
walk on stormy seas speaking but just a whisper to hush
the winds that swept so violently about Him. These feet
would walk the dusty roads of heartache and betrayal
finding no place to rest but only a wooden cross of
suffering and shame. These same feet that had trod where
angels had would bow to wash the very feet of the one
who would betray Him. These feet that traveled so far
coming all the way from glory so that we might walk with
Him there someday.

It's at these feet that the world fades away and eternity
slips into view. The place where all war ceases because
the battle you find is already won. The feet where angels
linger and never cease to cry "holy, holy, holy" is the
Lamb who was slain before the foundation of the world.

6

There at these feet you'll find the nail pierce markings of the One who died for you. Precious are these feet for they bear the marks of love eternal. Love that longs for the day to hold your face in His nail pierced hands and say welcome home.

In a world of confusion, constant turmoil, valleys of suffering and great hostility there is but one place to find comfort, strength and guidance for every moment and circumstance of life, the feet of Jesus. At the feet of Jesus storms quiet and the roaring waves of life cease settling the wind swept soul. At the feet of Jesus I find myself at home. I find a tower of strength and a bulwark that will never ever fail me. A place where I am accepted and loved for there are no secrets there. A place where I too must linger and stay a while with the lover of my soul, captivated by His presence and His holiness. I am His and He is mine and I am in need of nothing or no one when I am with Him, for He fully satisfies. He knows my name for I see it there inscribed on the palm of His hands. No other place will do but the feet of Jesus for it is the highest place in heaven. It's the place you were created to occupy.

This study you are taking will be no ordinary study but rather a journey to a place. This journey we'll take together, you & I, will be a journey to the very feet of Jesus Himself. We will see the secret treasures found there that the world does not know of. If the world knew of them they would give up all possessions that they might seek them out and claim them as their very own. It's not a prize to be won or a goal to strive for, but rather it is a birthright that any heir of the throne hath right and privilege to. We will see what drives us to His feet and what keeps us there. We will find the joy of worship, sweet peace of mind, and rest of soul. Since the beginning of time men have searched for the secret of life. To find the secret to life one must find the secret place where true life begins. This secret place is here at the sweet feet of Jesus.

Before we begin I want to ask you to take a moment and complete your "pre-journey" assignment that is provided. These are questions that will take some time of meditation before answering so, please don't rush to answer them but give them time to settle in over your mind and into your heart. We will come back to this assignment at the end of this study. Thank you for your commitment in being a good student of God's Word. I am praying for you that God will open your eyes, that you may know what is the hope of His calling for you. And in the knowing answer loudly, "here I am Lord" what would you have thy servant to do.

Pre-Journey Assignment

1. If you could have God do one thing in your life what would it be?

_____

_____

_____

_____

_____

2. Why would you want God to do this?

_____

_____

_____

_____

3. If God did this one thing in your life how would it affect those closest to you or those who are around you everyday?

_____

_____

_____

4. Why do you think God hasn't done this one thing for you?

_____

_____

_____

_____

_____

Write out a prayer to God in the space provided below asking God what you want Him to do in your life through this course. Share with Him your heart's desire. Then I will meet you on day one.

Dear God,

Sitting At His Feet

There I was a scraggly haired, freckled face, wide-eyed little girl sprawled comfortably on the floor in front of the big comfy chair. With scraped up knees from climbing up the Magnolia tree and my face all smudged with dirt, there I sat waiting and watching at the feet of beloved papa. Sometimes I would sit for hours anxiously waiting for him to finish reading his newspaper that would tell him of the events of the day. I knew from experience, as did the other grandchildren, that when papa finished reading his newspaper he would get up from his favorite chair.

What was so important about him getting up from his chair you might ask? You see, my papa ran a laundry route on which he took me along many times. Because he ran a laundry route he would come home with pockets full of change! We grandkids all knew that when papa sat down in his chair some of his change always made its way down into the pockets of the chair. Once he got up I was allowed to have any change that I found. This was papa's rule and we loved it. He loved to make us wait, for this was his entertainment.

I sat there as little girl wide eyed with wonder because I knew that if I waited long enough I would walk away richer than when I came. I recognized the benefit of being there. I believe it is much the same way in the story we are going to study this week. Our story is the story of Mary and her sister Martha. This is a familiar story to many but oh the treasures that are to be dug out in the marvelous encounter with Jesus.

11

Before you begin each day's lesson please take a moment and ask God to speak to your heart. Ask Him to take you to the very feet of Jesus and help you to listen to what He would have to say to you. Ask Him to "open your mind to understand the scriptures" (Luke 24:45). This study will be a time for you to sit at His feet as His little girl anticipating something wonderful to be given just to you.

- Open your Bible and read all of Luke Chapter 10. This will give you a full understanding of the events that led up to the passage of scripture that we will be looking at today. The book of Luke is unique in that unlike the other Gospels it is written in Chronological order. This makes following the life of Jesus a little easier for the reader seeking to understand the order of events.

- Now that you have finished reading through Luke chapter 10, I want you to read Luke 10:38-42, which will be our primary focus this week and familiarize yourself with the story. For your convenience it is typed out for you at the end of this lesson, right after day four. I have used the NAS version for continuity because it's easy to understand and in my opinion does not compromise the scriptures. Once you have read through it I want you to go back and read through it once more but this time I want you to highlight every reference to Mary in blue. This will help her name stand out to us when we go back to observe what the text is saying. Remember this includes any pronouns referring to her as well.

- Once you've marked every reference to Mary answer the following questions:

In this passage where do we see Mary?

_____

_____

What was Mary doing? (hint: there were two things)

Mary was:_____

Mary was:_____

Jesus was traveling about and one day He came into the village of Bethany. Into the home of two sisters Martha and Mary, who had a brother named Lazarus. Bethany was a village on the southeastern slopes of the Mount of Olives and was only about two miles (three kilometers) east of Jerusalem near the road to Jericho. It was the place of some of the most important events of Jesus' life.

Can you imagine having Jesus in your home sitting comfortably there in front of you and talking to you? You and I, as hard as we may try, could never imagine what it must have been like having the Lord Himself sitting in our home visiting with us in human form. What a marvelous visitation of providence. What was it about this man that captivated Mary so? I believe we get a glimpse of the reason as we look further into the words of the text. I call these word windows and you'll see why in just a moment.

Word Windows

In the back of your lesson book you will find a section entitled Word Window. There you will find a list of the words, along with their meanings, that we will be studying during the course of this study. Turn there and locate the words **sitting** and **listening.** Once you've located them write their meanings in the place provided for you below. At the beginning of the Word Windows section you find some information that will be beneficial to you in understanding word studies and also how to do independent word studies on your own. It would be very beneficial for you to read this section before looking up your words.

Word studies are so beneficial to Bible study. It's like opening up a window; once they are opened they show us a whole different view. Take a moment to read over these two words and their definitions that you have written below and meditate on them. Once I find the meaning of a word I will take that meaning and incorporate it with the scripture the next time I read it through. This helps to expound the scriptures.

Sitting (KJV-sat) _____

_____

_____

_____

Listening (KJV-heard) _____

_____

_____

_____

- In the light of these meanings why do you think Mary might have been sitting at the feet of Jesus?

  _____

  _____

- We know whom she was listening to, but **what** was she listening to?

  Mary was listening to the _____ of Jesus.

- What are some ways that we might listen to the words of Jesus today? Make a list below.

  _____

  _____

  _____

- Read verse 42 again in this passage and answer the following questions:

  a. What was the *"one thing"* that was necessary that Jesus was referring to?

  _____

  _____

  b. List every thing you learn about this *"one thing"* on the space provided.
  (Hint there are 4)

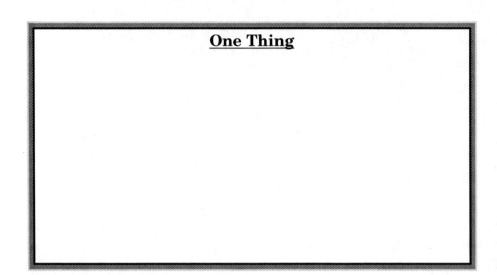

One Thing

In case you didn't find all four I will share them with you.

"ONE THING"

- It is necessary
- It is good
- It's a choice
- Can't be taken away from us

PRINCIPLE

RECOGNIZE THE BENEFIT OF BEING AT THE FEET OF JESUS.

Ecclesiastes 5:1 says... *"draw near to listen"*. I believe that Mary recognized the benefit of being at the feet of Jesus. She had a heart that wanted to not just listen to the words of Jesus, but she very much wanted to understand them. We learn in this passage that Jesus Himself said that being at His feet and listening to His word was a choice, for Mary had chosen it. Jesus never intends to force us to come but rather that we would choose from the heart to be at His feet. Jesus called this a good choice on Mary's part. Jesus also said that it was necessary for us to sit at His feet and listen to His word. He even says further that it is the only thing that we really need.

Mary encountered Jesus in a personal way even though she never spoke a word. By being at His feet Mary showed that she had recognized the following Truths about herself:

- She needed Jesus
- She needed to listen to His Word

What is gained while sitting at His feet can never be taken away from us. The world cannot take from us what it did not give to us.

฿ENEFIT

SITTING AT THE FEET OF JESUS WE FIND OURSELVES IN A PLACE OF ETERNAL VALUE.

Being at the feet of Jesus is no ordinary place to be. It is a place that will bring eternal value to our lives. See this in scripture with me as you look up the following verses noting what they teach us about eternity.

- Look up and read Matthew 24:35

According to this verse, what will pass away and what will not pass away?

_____

_____

_____

His Word is eternal isn't it? So when we are listening to His Words we can know that they are Words that will never ever pass away for they are eternal. I John 2:17 also tells us that the world is passing away but we can know that even when the world is gone His Word will still remain. Why wouldn't we want to listen?

- Look up and read Hebrews 13:8-14 and answer the following questions. Although these may seem like difficult scriptures, don't get weighed down by the things you may not understand. Some of these things we will discuss in the teaching session.

Will Jesus ever change?

_____

No matter what happens in the world around you, past, present or future, Jesus will never change. You can turn on the news on any given day and you will find the world constantly changing, physically, emotionally, spiritually, philosophically, and the list goes on and on. Your life could change forever in just a moment but Jesus is a constant.

According to verse 9 in this passage what is good for the heart?

_____

_____

_____

Based on these verses, are we to seek the things of eternity or things that are temporal? (Hint: verse 14 uses a city to teach us this truth)

_____

_____

_____

Personal Evaluation

Do you want your life to count for eternity?

_____

_____

If you answered yes, and I pray that you did, then I would say to you my precious friend; "sit at the feet of Jesus". Listening takes a concentrated effort that comes from desperation to know and understand. You must come to the place of stillness, when all else quiets around you and all distractions have faded from view and your eyes are fixed straight upon the Master's face.

Are you desperate to know Jesus?

_____

If you are not desperate to know Jesus then you do not
care about eternity or that your life count for eternity.
These two actions are linked together and you will not
have one without the other.

Do you recognize the benefit of being at His feet?

_____

_____

What response, what change, would God want from you in
the light of these personal evaluation questions? Truth
always demands a response from the one it was given to.

This is all, my precious friend. Will you stop and pray
right now with me and ask the Holy Spirit, the Spirit of
Truth, to lead and teach you during your time in this
study? Ask Him to speak to your heart and reveal words
of truth from His Word, opening your eyes that you may
behold wonderful things? Would you ask the Holy Spirit
to do a work so deep and thorough that when you come to
the end of this journey you will find that there is a
different person finishing than the one who began? Only
God can change us and only the Holy Spirit can reveal
truth. May Jesus do above and beyond all that you could
ever think or hope as you sit at His feet.

There are literally millions of books on the market, hundreds of TV shows, radio shows and programs that give lots of varied opinions on a host of topics from relationships to jobs to health to politics and religion and so on. There is plenty to listen to. I have found that the world is a noisy place. Unfortunately most of what is being heard by the world is from the world and is not from God nor accepted by God. Yesterday we looked at Mary sitting at the feet of Jesus. We found that she was not just sitting at His feet but she was listening to His words. Although so much was going on around her, what caused her to tune everything else out and devote her attention to this man and the words He was speaking? We know that His words will never pass away but what other things can we learn that made His words so important, so different than anything else she had ever heard? If we do not understand the importance of Jesus' words we will never be willing to sit and listen to them. Why are His words so "necessary" for us? This will be our topic of study today.

Look up the following verses and once you've read them list out beside each one what you learned about the words of Jesus.

- John 6:63-69

_____

_____

_____

- John 12:44-50

_____

_____

- Luke 24:24-32 – (Jesus has just risen from the dead)

_____

_____

_____

- Look up John 17:4-8

  Whose words did Jesus speak?

_____

_____

We know from these verses that Jesus spoke the words of God. Look up the following verses and write down what you discover about the word of God. There are so many verses on this subject that time would not permit for an exhaustive study so I have listed only a few.

- Psalm 12:6

_____

_____

_____

- Psalm 19:7-8

_____

_____

_____

- Psalm 119:105

_____

_____

- Proverbs 30:5

_____

_____

- In Luke 9:35 God is speaking, what did He say for them to do? Write out what God said word for word.

_____

I want you to memorize this scripture this week and be ready to say it to at least one person before you come to our lesson time together. It's a simple verse and easy to learn. Remember when the Word is stored in your heart's chamber no one can take it from you. This is a powerful verse to put to memory.

One more verse for today and we will be finished. Look up and read carefully **Colossians 1:12-20** then answer the questions.

- According to these verses, why should we pay attention to the words of Jesus?

_____

_____

- What place did Jesus come to hold?

_____

From God's Word we see that Jesus speaks the Words of God and God Himself commands us to listen to His

Words. We have seen with our own eyes that He has been given first place above everyone and everything.

PRINCIPLE

RECOGNIZE THE AUTHORITY OF HIS WORD.

I believe that Mary must have believed that there was something very special about this man they called Jesus. Could she have had any idea she was sitting at the very feet of God? I do know that something must have burned within her when He was speaking for we see her sitting, quietly listening to His every word. The power of His Word spoken to our hearts will captivate us. Has your heart ever burned within you at the hearing of the Word of God? Do you recognize the authority of the Word of God in your own life? Do you feel compelled to listen and understand the Word of God, or have you ever given it any thought? Is the Word of God personal to you?
You will not live by the Word of God if you do not view it as the standard by which we are to live. Once you have bowed the knee in recognition to God's Word as supreme authority in your life you will reap a marvelous benefit.

BENEFIT

YOU WILL NEVER BE MISLED

Have you ever been confused or perplexed over a situation or over a decision you had to make. How many times have you said: "I don't know what to do?" Have you ever had a child that you just did not know how to handle as a parent? Have you ever been confused by another's teaching, or maybe by something you've seen on television wondering; "is this for real or is this from God or not"? Maybe you are struggling with unforgiveness, bitterness, wrong relationships, or a sin in your life you just can't get victory over. God's Word will never mislead you. People can mislead you, emotions can mislead you, circumstances can mislead you but God's Word never will. God's Word is sure proof, tried and tested (Proverbs 30:5).

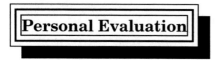

Personal Evaluation

When you make decisions, big or small, on what basis do you make those decisions?

_____

_____

_____

Is there anything or anyone in your life right now that does not line up with what you know God's Word says? If so write it out in the space below. Seeing it in front of you is extremely helpful because it confronts us in a very personal way.

_____

_____

_____

_____

_____

How is the authority of the Word of God seen in your life by others?

_____

_____

_____

Do you view the Word of God as Supreme Authority over everyone everywhere in any and every situation or just over those who believe in God? Explain your answer.

_____

_____

_____

_____

Is there any thing or anyone else that you have put in the same place of authority in your life as the Word of God? If so, list them and explain why in the space below. This question is extremely important so take some time to think on it before you answer.

_____

_____

_____

_____

_____

_____

You've worked so hard today and I'm very proud of you. You are sitting at the feet of Jesus, because you have been in His word. Have you been listening to what He is saying to you? How I have prayed for you that these Principles will grip your very soul and anchor you into a constant communion with the Lord Himself. May you bind them round about your heart and let them sink there deeply and eternally. His truths will never mislead you. I will see you tomorrow!

So far we have seen truths from God's Word that have shown us that there are great benefits from being at the feet of Jesus because of who He is and the power and authority of His Word. Today we're going to look at the other sister, Martha. Read through our passage of scripture of study (Luke 10:38-42) once more. This time as you read I want you to highlight every reference to Martha in yellow. We want to be able to distinguish the two sisters very easily when we read through this passage. Once you have finished I want you to list below everything you learned about sister Martha.

```
┌─────────────────────────────────────────────┐
│                  Martha                       │
│                                               │
│                                               │
│                                               │
│                                               │
│                                               │
│                                               │
│                                               │
│                                               │
│                                               │
│                                               │
│                                               │
└─────────────────────────────────────────────┘
```

In the light of our passage of scripture in Luke Chapter 10, answer the following questions:

- Who invited Jesus into the home?

- In verse 40 what do we see Martha doing?

_____

_____

_____

- What was Martha's complaint to Jesus? Write her complaint out **word for word** below.

Martha's Complaint

_____
_____
_____

- In verse 41 Jesus tells Martha what her problem is. What was Jesus' reply? Write it out word for word in the space provided for you below.

Jesus Response to Martha's Complaint

_____
_____
_____

Did you notice that Jesus never addressed the complaint or the request that Martha made?

You see Martha thought her problem was Mary, but Jesus told her that it wasn't Mary at all. What Jesus basically said to Martha was that the problem she was having was no one's fault but her own! You may be saying; "Pam, does the Lord really do that to us?" Of course He does! The truth, that's usually the last thing we want to hear isn't it? We are blame shifters by nature. We blame it on our circumstances, on other people and even on the Lord Himself at times. Jesus lovingly but authoritatively shared with Martha that what was concerning her was not something she needed to be concerned with at all. But Jesus also taught her the right thing to be concerned with and that was with His Word.

- If you had to tell what the difference between Martha and Mary was, what you would you say?

_____

_____

_____

_____

_____

Go back to the text and underline with a pen the first five words of Martha's statement to Jesus. Once you've done that come back and write these first five words that Martha spoke to the Lord in verse 40 in the blanks below.

_____ _____ _____ _____ _____.

30

Just looking at these first five words that Martha spoke to Jesus what do you think her opinion of Jesus toward her was?

_____

_____

- What were the things that kept Martha from being at the feet of Jesus?

_____

_____

If I were to ask you to write down all the things that can keep people from sitting at the feet of Jesus and from listening to His Word, what would you list? It could be all those things that keep us from Church, reading our Bibles, praying, daily devotional times, etc... I believe that there are many reasons, many excuses but I believe that there are things at the heart of why we choose to let these things come between us and our time with the Lord and listening and learning His Word.

Martha's view was that she really didn't think that the Lord cared for her because He wasn't doing anything to help her situation. Have you ever felt that way about God? Because He didn't give you what you wanted, what you asked for and so He must not care about you? Martha did, because she goes on further to tell the Lord to do something about Mary because she wasn't helping her with the work. How many times have we gone to the Lord in prayer only to tell Him what we want Him to do for us? Like Martha we find ourselves doing all the talking and never listening to what He wants to say to us. Martha was having a pity party to say the least. Jesus didn't even respond to the accusation that He didn't care or that

31

she had been left alone to do the work. Jesus wasn't concerned with the accusation because He knew it wasn't true. But Jesus did give Martha some wonderful advice for her situation didn't He? He showed her that she had two problems that prevented her from doing the same thing that Mary was doing.

Can you list what these two things were?

"Martha Martha, you are _____ and _____ by so many things."

We will look further into these words tomorrow but for now, as you read this passage one has to wonder did Martha listen to Jesus when He gave her this advice. She had not been listening thus far but was she listening when Jesus addressed her personally? When it was a word from Him just for her and her alone?

Let's look and see. Read John 12:1-3. We're going to be studying this even later in our study but for now I just want you to focus on these two verses. Time has passed since Jesus was in Mary and Martha's home. What do you see Martha doing compared to what Mary was doing? Had Martha listened?

_____

Oh how God wants us to listen! We are usually so busy telling the Lord what we want or what is wrong that we never ask Him if He has anything He wants to say to us. By nature we want to be heard rather than want to listen. Listening is difficult and challenging especially when we are bothered and concerned with many things. It's obvious that Martha was a worker isn't it? God loves a hard worker and hard work is not a sin. But God desires something more from us than just our service. Just from the encounter with Mary and Jesus in Luke Chapter 10 we see what it is, we see a dynamic truth a life changing principle:

PRINCIPLE

WE'RE NOT TO BE ABOUT THE WORK OF THE LORD BUT ABOUT THE LORD OF THE WORK.

Duties, positions, distractions, all these things will come and go but the words of Jesus make lasting imprints into our lives. It is possible to be in Jesus' presence and not know Him. He told His disciples in John 14:9 *"have I been with you so long and thou has not known me"*

How sad these words must have been to the disciples. How sad they must have been for Jesus to speak them. You see Martha invited Jesus into her home. Yet she did not find herself in His presence. Like Martha, many of us invite Jesus into our presence but we never come into His. Martha saw Jesus as a guest of the house whereas Mary saw Him as Lord of the house. How often has Jesus been in our midst yet we did not give Him recognition? Do you treat Jesus as a guest, someone to work and labor over, or do you honor him as your Lord, someone you bow to and acknowledge?

What is your opinion about the Lord concerning you? Do believe He truly cares for you?
When we are about the Lord of the work and not about the work itself what a wonderful benefit that will flood into our lives.

𝔅ENEFIT

STRIVING CEASES

Look up Psalm 46:10 and write out that first sentence of this verse in the space below:

_____

In the King James version the verse is translated "be still", in the NAS it is "Cease Striving". The truth we have learned in today's lesson is seen so beautifully from the words of the Psalmist. When we are still before Him there is no strife. Strife is what keeps us from being still before Him. We live in a world that is always in a hurry! There's no time to be still in the age we live in, or is there? Strife is and worry is a major contributor to health problems, relationships and many other things. What's the answer? Sitting at the feet of Jesus is the only answer. We have seen with our own eyes this week that when we sit at the feet of Jesus and we concern ourselves with Him and Him alone all strife fades, it ceases to exist. Strife cannot stay in the presence of Jesus.

Personal Evaluation

Have you been so busy with serving the Lord that you have no time for Him?

_____

Is your life characterized by the Lord or by the work you do for the Lord?

_____

Is there strife in your life?

_____

_____

When was the last time you were still before the Lord in total silence?

_____

_____

The Lord desires intimacy with us, not a labor detail. He wants to see us at His feet.

Do you know why? Because one who is intimate with Jesus will never leave impressions of himself but rather an eternal imprint of the face of God upon the lives they encounter. Pride disappears when you are humbled before the throne of Grace. May people not be impressed with your work for the Lord, but rather with the Lord you work for.

Meditate on these truths and I will see you tomorrow.
Thank you for your hard work in doing your study today.
I'm very proud of you.

DAY FOUR

Yesterday we saw that Martha had worries and bothers or distractions that kept her from being at the feet of Jesus. Much like Martha we too often find our lives spinning un-seemingly out of control. Our duties and commitments have us enslaved and joy is nowhere to be found. Today I want us to see and recognize the enemies of being at the feet of Jesus. Let's begin by reading through our text of study once more in Luke 10 to refresh your memory; I want this passage to be engraved upon your heart. Once you've done that I want you turn to the Word Windows section in the back of your workbook and locate the words below and write down their definitions beside each one in the place provided for you below:

Distracted (KJV-cumbered) _____

_____

_____

_____

Worried (KJV-careful) _____

_____

_____

_____

Bothered (KJV-troubled) _____

_____

_____

_____

We've been studying Martha all week but based on the meanings of these word windows how would you now describe the life of Martha and the reasons why she was not at the feet of Jesus that day?

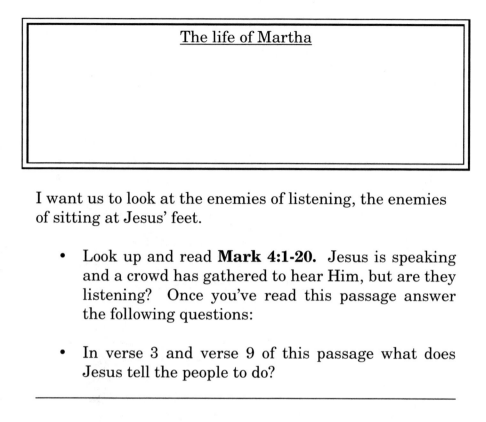

The life of Martha

I want us to look at the enemies of listening, the enemies of sitting at Jesus' feet.

- Look up and read **Mark 4:1-20.** Jesus is speaking and a crowd has gathered to hear Him, but are they listening? Once you've read this passage answer the following questions:

- In verse 3 and verse 9 of this passage what does Jesus tell the people to do?

_____

_____

- According to verses 17 & 19 what are the things that Jesus says will keep us from receiving the Word of God?

_____

_____

_____

Two times Jesus calls the people to listen or harken which means to pay attention to or take heed to. I believe that what Jesus was about to tell them He really wanted them to understand don't you? He wanted them, you and I to know the things that will rob us of listening and receiving

the Word of God. I'm always convicted by these words especially; *"the desire for other things enter in"*...
Do you know what the number one enemy is of being at the feet of Jesus? What keeps you from spending time with Him? It's the desire for other things. Paul said of Demus, that he had deserted them *"having loved his present world"*. The desire for other things, the draw or pull of duties, careers, busyness, worries, anxieties, all these are enemies of time spent with the Lord.

If you had to rate your time spent with Jesus not counting church services how do you think you would measure up? Using the table that follows. Read the choices and then check the one that best describes you.

ME

I spend at least one hour a day praying and reading my Bible.	
I spend about 30 minutes a day praying or reading my Bible	
I kind of hit or miss with reading my Bible and praying. Some days I do and some days I don't.	
I rarely spend any time with the Lord. Only when a crisis arises. The only time I read my Bible is when I am at Church.	

The first step to any problem solving is to first recognize that there is a problem and second is identifying what the problem is. Third should be, understanding how to correct the problem. But first we must always recognize the problem.

PRINCIPLE

RECOGNIZE THE ENEMIES OF TIME SPENT AT THE FEET OF JESUS.

Make a list below of the things, people, activities, etc. that keep you from being at the feet of Jesus:

Things that keep me from sitting at the feet of Jesus

There is so much in the world today to vie for our attention, demand our time and exhaust our energy. Maybe you are one of the many others in the world today that give themselves to so many other things that there is just no strength left to give to the Lord to spend time with Him. What is your hearts desire? Do you want to be a Mary; one who is at total peace, finding everything you will ever want or need in Jesus? Or would you rather be a Martha, tired, busy, bothered and weighed down with the burdens of life leaving no time to spend with Jesus, missing the one thing you need the most? I think I know how we would all answer that question. Common sense would cry out MARY, I want to be a MARY! If that's your hearts desire, then don't settle by becoming or remaining

39

a MARTHA. Remember Jesus told us that Mary made the choice to be with Him. What choice is God prompting you to make concerning the time you spend with Him?

Will we find you months, even years from now still busy and occupied by so many things and find Jesus still sitting and waiting for you to come to Him? I pray you will make a Godly choice right this moment that will forever change your life. It will change everything about you and about your life, the way you see it and the way you see others. I truly believe that misery of life comes only from one that is void of Jesus! A life void of personal time spent with Him.

The hardest part is recognizing the things that keep us from Him. The things that we have allowed to enslave us, to manipulate our time, our thoughts and exhaust our energies. The things that we have allowed to order our day, to dictate our time. Recognize these things and begin to deal with them one by one and you will see the benefit of it.

BENEFIT

JESUS WILL BE MY PRIORITY

Priorities are an issue for all of us. If I never recognize the enemies that keep me from being at the feet of Jesus then Jesus will never become my priority. Jesus as we learned earlier this week from the book of Colossians is to have first place in everything. In other words, Jesus is to have first place in your life and no one or nothing is to come before Him. This is God's will, that Jesus be first.

Personal Evaluation

If you had to make a list of the priorities in your life in order of importance what would be at the top of the list? Why don't you join me right now and make a list of the priorities in your life in the order of importance. To help you make this list think on the things that take up most of your time, the things that weigh heaviest on your mind and heart. What are the things that you live for or look forward to every day? Base this on action rather than emotions. For example, we may say my family is my number one priority but they may be last on my list if listed by the amount of time I spend with them. So make your priority list based on action (reality) not on how you say you feel.

My Priorities

- Was Jesus at the top of your list?

Prioritizing isn't easy is it? God wants to have first place in your life or He wouldn't have led you to take this study. How He loves you, precious student of His Word. God's heart is not to shame you but to correct you and give you His best for your life.

What is it that God would have you change in your life in order to make Him first?

_____

_____

_____

Studying God's Word is not just about learning but rather it's about changing.

Review your memory verse and make sure you are ready to say it to a friend this week in our WOW teaching session. That's all for this week. It's been a wonderful start so far hasn't it? Let's review the Truths that God has taught us and the benefits we receive from them. Ask God to seer them upon your heart. Remember these are life-changing principles with Life giving benefits.

Week In Review

Principle	Benefit
Recognize the benefit of being at His feet	A Place of Eternal Value
Recognize the Authority of His Word	You will never be misled
Be about the Lord of the work not the work of the Lord	Striving Ceases
Recognize the Enemies of time spent with Jesus	Priorities in order

May I invite you to have a seat at the feet of Jesus and may you linger there for a while

NOTES

Luke 10:38-42

38. Now as they were traveling along, He entered a village; and a woman named Martha welcomed Him into her home.

39. She had a sister called Mary, who was seated at the Lord's feet, listening to His word.

40. But Martha was distracted with all her preparations; and she came up to Him and said, "Lord do you not care that my sister has left me to do all the serving alone? Then tell her to help me."

41. But the Lord answered and said to her, "Martha, Martha, you are worried and bothered about so many things;

42. But only one thing is necessary, for Mary has chosen the good part, which shall not be taken away from her."

The Place Emptying

The men had been fishing all through the night, casting their nets out over the waters of Lake Gennesaret or more commonly known as the Sea of Galilee, but there would be no fish found in their nets come morning light. Tired and hungry as the sun came up they landed their boats up on the shore and began to wash out their nets as they had done so many times before, for this was the life of a fisherman. But that morning would be different from every other morning, for Jesus had come upon their shores. As was His custom Jesus was teaching to the crowd of people that had gathered around Him to listen. Then Jesus did an unusual thing, He climbed into the boat of Simon Peter and asked Peter to put the boat out a little way from the land, away from the crowd. From this day forward Peter's life would never be the same.

Do you remember the day you met Jesus? The very first time that you encountered Him in a very real and personal way, the moment that He changed your life forever? Is this a day that is real to you? This is a day that was very real to a little fisherman named Simon whom the Lord called Peter. Peter would become one of Jesus' greatest fishermen! Why? Because Peter had a life changing moment when he fell at the feet of Jesus. This life changing moment will be our course of study this week, and oh what a week it's going to be for you if you will persevere and work diligently through your lesson. Why don't you stop and kneel before the Teacher Himself and ask Him to speak to your heart in a personal way as you study His word, asking Him to change you as you sit at His feet that your life may never be the same.

Turn to the last page of this week's lesson and read through **Luke 5:1-11** which is typed out for you there. This will be our focus of study this week. What a powerful encounter this was in the life of Simon Peter. As you read through the text take your time and soak up the scene that is taking place. When you've finished I will meet you back here.

- Now that you've finished reading through the passage of scripture I want you to go back through it once more but this time I want you to highlight Simon Peter and every reference to Simon Peter in blue. There will be some places that will refer to more than one person that includes Peter (like the words them & they). I want you to mark these in the same way because Simon Peter is included in these references. Once you've finished highlighting all the references to Peter answer the following questions.

- This may sound simple but, what was Simon Peter by trade?

_____

- Whose boat did Jesus get into and what did Jesus continue doing once He got into the boat?

_____

_____

- What was Simon doing when Jesus first saw him? (hint: verse 2)

_____

_____

In verse 3, Jesus asked Simon to put out his boat a little way from the land. Once Jesus had finished teaching there were two things that Jesus told Simon to do. You can find these easily if you will take a red pen and while reading through the text draw a cross symbol over every reference that is made to Jesus. Once you've found these fill in the blanks in the sentence below.

Put out _____ ___ **deep** _____ **and** ____

your _____ ___ ___ _____.

The first thing Jesus did was call Peter away from the shores of the ordinary. He called him away from the crowd. Isn't it interesting to see that there were only two things that Jesus told Peter to do? They were very simple things, and they were things that Peter could do for he had done them many times before. Ordinary chores done on no ordinary day would change the course of this fisherman's life forever and others as well. What made this encounter so life-changing? I believe it will help us tremendously to see the answer if we will back up in time before this day and examine the life of Peter. Was this Peter's first encounter with Jesus? I want to take you to a couple of passages that will give you the answer. Look up the following scriptures and answer the questions listed.

- Matthew 8:14-15
  What do we see Jesus doing?

  _____

  _____

  _____

  _____

- Luke 4: 38-39

  This is the same event but I wanted to take you to Matthew first because it establishes that this Simon mentioned here in Luke chapter four is Simon Peter the fishermen.

- How did Peter encounter Jesus?

  _____

  _____

- In this scene what did Jesus do in the life of Peter?

  _____

  _____

- Does the scripture give us any indication that this was a life changing event for Peter?

  _____

  _____

There is one other place that I want to take you to. Turn in your Bible to John 1: 29-42. John the Baptist is announcing Jesus. As you read this passage note what you learn about Peter. This is the very first time that Peter meets Jesus. Was this a life-changing event for Peter? Are we told in this passage that Peter acknowledged Jesus is any way?

  _____

Continue reading in John Chapter 2 verses 1-11. This is Jesus' very first miracle that we know of that He performed publicly. What a marvelous scene as we see the Lord take six ordinary stone water pots filled with water and turn it into wine at a wedding in Cana.

Did this encounter with Jesus have any affect on the disciples?

_____

_____

Do you think it was a life-changing encounter? Explain your answer.

_____

_____

There are two words in this passage that I want us to take a closer look at. They are listed below for you. Look up each one in your word window section and write out their meanings beside each in the space provided for you.

Glory _____

_____

_____

_____

Believed _____

_____

_____

_____

Peter was present at this wedding for the scriptures tell us that Jesus' disciples were with Him. In the light of these word windows, do you think this encounter with Jesus was a life changing one for Peter? Why or why not?

Explain your answer.

_____

_____

This does give us something to think about doesn't it? We know that Peter had encountered Jesus before the day at the shores of Galilee. We know that the Lord had performed a miracle right before his very eyes. We know that Jesus healed his mother-in-law. Peter knew of Jesus' healing powers, and he had witnessed Jesus' manifested glory at the wedding and scriptures tell us that he even believed in Jesus. If all these things are true then why was this encounter at sea so powerful that we see Peter fall at Jesus' feet? So powerful that we see Peter's life change forever. Why had he not fallen at His feet before? Surely someone turning the water into wine would be reason enough, or healing a loved one in your own home would warrant a reverential bowing.

What was so different this morning? This is what I believe God wants to show us this week as we dwell together on the shores of Galilee with a fisherman whom Jesus called Peter. Rest now, you've worked hard and there is much to meditate upon. I pray that you will seek God for answers to the questions I have asked you for I believe they are life changing for all who find them and embrace them. Bye for now precious student.

On day one of this week's study we were left with some thought provoking questions. Today we will return back to our passage of study found in Luke Chapter 5 and see if we can begin to unlock some of the answers. Let's turn there and read through the passage to refresh our minds. A good habit of Bible study is to read and re-read a passage until it becomes ingrained deep within. As you read I want you to find and underline in a color of your choice the words that Peter spoke to Jesus. Once you've located and marked them, write out the words that Peter spoke to Jesus in verse 5.

Simon answered and said, "_____

_____

                                                                                    "
_____

How did Peter address Jesus in verse 5?

_____

_____

_____

Turn to your "Word Windows" section in the back of your workbook and find the word Master. Once you've located it write down it's meaning in the space provided for you.

Master _____

_____

_____

_____

Just from what Peter calls Jesus in this verse, what do you think Peter's opinion of Jesus was at this point?

_____

_____

Jesus made a request to Peter in verse 4 and Peter responded to this request in verse 5. I want you to write down the request and the response in the space provided.

Jesus Request   **Peter's Response**

Peter told the Lord that they had been fishing all night long and had caught nothing but that he would let down his nets anyway.

Notice the words of Jesus here: *"let down your nets for a catch"*

- Why were they to let down their nets?

_____

_____

Notice the words of response from Peter here: *"I will let down the nets"*.

- Was Peter letting down his nets for a catch or only to appease Jesus?

_____

_____

_____

Peter never intended to catch any fish when he let down his nets because he and the others had been trying to catch some fish all night long and yet they had caught nothing. Besides, in this particular place and with this type of fishing, the deep waters were not the place to cast your nets if you wanted to catch any fish and your boats need to be closer into the shores in the shallow waters, not out from the land, all facts which Peter knew. I imagine Peter and the others were extremely tired and weary, because fishing with nets is laborious and exhausting. Can't you just almost hear what Peter must have been thinking? He had been up all night and I'm sure all that he wanted to do at this point was to clean up his nets, go home, shower, eat a good home cooked meal and then get some much needed rest. Then along comes a teacher that thinks He can tell him how to catch fish. Peter had been doing this all his life. This was his trade, he was the professional. What could this man called Jesus possibly know about catching fish, after all everyone knew He was the son of a carpenter? Peter was only letting down his net out of respect for a man who he referred to as "teacher". He was just trying to be obedient out of mere respect. After all, this teacher had healed his mother-in-law and He had even turned water into wine at a wedding.

I believe that Jesus chose that shoreline that day and I believe that He chose that particular boat. The scriptures tell us here that there were two boats on the shore that day and yet Jesus chose Peter's boat. It was no accident that Peter and the others had caught nothing all night long. It wasn't because of bad luck that they came back with empty nets that day but rather providence. God allows us to fail sometimes to bring about a marvelous visitation. It is through failure many times that God gives life changing revelation. Jesus' purpose in choosing Peter's boat was not to show Peter how to catch fish. I believe Jesus wanted to show Peter something much greater. He wanted to show them His fullness. He wanted to show them Himself and He used the one thing that a fisherman would understand. A fisherman's net means everything to him for without it he could not catch fish. Without it he could not feed or support his family. That net was his life. A fisherman could do without his boat but he could never do without his net. So why did Jesus allow their nets to be drawn up empty that night? I believe it was to show them their emptiness by showing them His fullness. He wanted them to know how empty their lives were and to reveal to them His magnificent fullness. We see our first biblical truth:

PRINCIPLE

WE CANNOT KNOW OUR EMPTINESS UNTIL WE SEE HIS FULLNESS.

What are we to compare our lives with? Today the influences of Hollywood, the media, the characters portrayed in the many popular television series, the music world, talk shows, and the ever growing list of motivational speakers are leaving many lives striving to be something that God never intended them to be. We are left with thoughts of: "If I only looked like that then I would be happy", "If I only had that kind of man in my life", "if only I had that much money all my problems would be solved", "if only I had that kind of house I know I would be happy", "if only I drove that kind of car", "if only I were popular", "if only I were that successful I wouldn't want anything else", and the "if only" goes on and on. These things, these lifestyles, will only leave us empty because we will never find true life in anything or in anyone else but Jesus Himself. How will we ever know if we are missing something if we do not compare our lives with the right thing? Peter had never seen his emptiness before this day because He had never really seen Jesus' fullness. The moment Peter saw his empty nets filled he saw the fullness of Jesus and the emptiness of his own life. What did finding out this marvelous truth do in the life of Peter?

BENEFIT

LIFE OVERFLOWING

How will we ever know our hands need to be filled if they were never found empty? You see Peter and the others would have been content with their lives just as they were. Sure they had the disappointment of coming back empty handed that morning. But, they never would have known how empty their lives really were if Jesus had not shown them how full it could be with Him. Jesus showed them what they were missing. Is it any wonder that Peter fell on his knees?

So often we think that Jesus only does these things for others and that He would never do them for us personally. Our mentality is that it's meant for everyone else and I will always be just a bystander. Up to this point Peter had only been a bystander, one watching from a distance at Jesus work miracles in the lives of others around him but never his own life. But here in the early morning hours Jesus did something just for Peter. He came to Peter's shoreline, He got into Peter's boat, He spoke directly to Peter and He filled Peter's nets and boat to overflowing. Jesus became real to Peter that day because Jesus affected Peter in a personal way.

To reinforce this truth, look up the following verses and note what you learn about Jesus and about life:

- John 10:10

_____

_____

- John 20:30-31

_____

_____

- John 1:1-14

_____

_____

According to verse 4 of this passage what is in Jesus?

_____

- Colossians 3:4: Paul is speaking to the Christians in the city of Colossae. What does he tell them about Jesus?

_____

_____

From these verses that you have just studied, where is life found?

_____

Can true life be found anywhere else?

_____

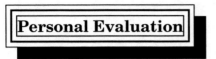

Personal Evaluation

Where are you looking to find joy? What do you think will make your life better, what will make your life full?

_____

_____

_____

Have you encountered Jesus in a very real and personal way or have you only been a spectator of Jesus watching Him work in the lives of others but never in your own life?

_____

_____

Explain why you answered yes or no to the previous question:

_____

_____

_____

Jesus' desire is not for us to watch how He changes the lives of others, never having ours changed by Him. But rather, He wants each of us to encounter Him, to know Him in a very real and personal way just as Peter did. Jesus is personal for He chose Peter's boat that day, just as He has chosen yours for you are doing this study! Jesus has just stepped into your boat, into your life. Through His very words He is revealing to you His fullness. And in seeing His fullness you, as Peter, will never, never be the same. How I pray that you will cast your empty net into the deep, deep waters of Him for they will never come up empty. It's only the empty nets that He chooses to fill.

I pray that you will let this powerful truth sink deep into your heart my dear friend. Let it settle in the deepest part. Truth comes little by little, line upon line. So be patient and be steadfast in your study.

Rest now, I will see you tomorrow.

Welcome back to another day of being on the shores of Galilee. Remember from day one we have seen that Jesus has come into Peter's life in a powerful and personal way. Once you've prayed turn in your Bible to Luke Chapter 4 and read through the entire chapter. This will help you understand the events that led up to the fishing scene that we have been studying. This will be our passage of study today and I want you to read through it once just to get your thoughts in focus before we begin our study. Once you have finished reading answer the following questions.

- What do you see Jesus doing in this chapter?

  _____

  _____

- What affect did He have, if any, on the lives of people He encountered?

  _____

  _____

In this chapter of Luke, Jesus comes into Nazareth and enters the Synagogue there. He opens up the Book of Isaiah and reads Isaiah 61:1. These words help us understand what Jesus' purpose was that day when he got into Peter's boat. I have typed out Isaiah 61:1 for you. Underline the reasons that Jesus gives for being sent by God.

Isaiah 61:1

"The Spirit of the Lord is upon me, Because He anointed Me to preach the Gospel to the poor. He has sent Me to proclaim release to the captives, and recovery of sight to the blind, to set free those who are oppressed. To proclaim the favorable year of the Lord."

- From this verse fill in the blanks of these sentences.

"He has sent me to _____ release to the _____, and _____ of _____ to the _____.

To set _____ those who are _____.

To proclaim the _____ year of the _____."

Out of these things which of these did Jesus do in the life of Peter in Luke 5?

_____

_____

I believe that Jesus came to open Peter's eyes to see who He was. I believe this because of the dialogue between Peter and Jesus. Let's look at it together. On day one we learned that Peter first addressed Jesus as "master" and

61

in our Word Window we learned that this word means "teacher". Read Luke 5:8 and answer the following questions:

- What did Peter do when he saw the great quantity of fish in their nets and in their boats?

_____

_____

Look again in Luke 5:8 and this time underline in a color of your choice the words that Peter cried to Jesus in verse 8. Once you've marked them write these words that Peter cried out at the feet of Jesus in the space provided:

"But when Simon Peter saw that, he fell down at Jesus' feet, saying,

_____

_____ "

- What title does Peter give Jesus this time?

_____

- In our previous passages of study had we ever seen a time or place where Peter had bowed the knee to Jesus and confessed Him as Lord?

_____

- Turn to your Word Windows section and look up the definition for Lord and record it in the space provided. I believe you will begin to see the depth of Peter's encounter with Jesus and why this was life changing once you see what this word means.

Look up and write out Psalm 45:11 in the space provided below. This is our memory verse for the week. It's simple to memorize but powerful.

_____

_____

_____

Because he is your Lord, bow down to Him. Up until this day Jesus was Lord but He was not Peter's Lord. Peter bowed the knee before the one whom he had only acknowledged as a great teacher and prophet, a great miracle worker. But Peter had never called Him Lord. Jesus went from being a teacher to supreme Lord in the eyes of Peter. This is why Peter went to his knees and cried out "Lord, O Lord". This was a cry from the deepest part of Peter. This encounter was so personal to Peter that it would forever be a symbol of revelation for him even after the Lord's resurrection from the dead. Read John 21: 1-12 and note the following:

- What did Peter do when he realized it was the Lord?

_____

_____

- What was the sign that revealed to them that it was the Lord?

_____

_____

- Did Jesus ever tell them that it was Him?

I believe that Jesus reveals Himself at times to us on a level that is often too deep for words. It's so personal that it's meant to be between you and Him. Peter knew it was Jesus because of the fish caught in the net. A personal sign between Him and Jesus, a loving reminder of the day He saw Jesus with opened eyes. The day His life changed forever. To see Jesus with open eyes means to see Him as supreme Lord and Savior.

Peter not only recognized Jesus as Lord, but Peter also recognized something about himself that day. Read through Peter's words once more that he cried out at the feet of Jesus. What did Peter acknowledge or cry out regarding himself?

Peter not only saw Jesus as Lord that day but he saw himself as a sinful man. Jesus has shown Peter his emptiness in the light of His fullness but then He revealed His Lordship by allowing Peter so see his sinfulness. There was another person that Peter saw that day with unveiled eye and that was himself. He needed no mirror for he was in the presence of Jesus and looking at Jesus will cause us to see ourselves. I believe that this is why we choose many times not to look at Jesus for who He really is because we don't want to see ourselves as we are. When Peter saw Himself he cried: *"depart from me Lord, Oh Lord, for I am a sinful man"*.

But when Peter looked into the mirror of his natural man apart from Christ he saw a man who was sinful and unworthy to be in the presence of Jesus. This was the moment that Peter was "born again".   This was the moment of eternal change.

PRINCIPLE

WE CANNOT ACKNOWLEDGE HIS LORDSHIP WITHOUT FIRST ACKNOWLEDGING OUR SINFULNESS.

We often want to skip over our sin and go straight to Jesus and the benefits that come from having Him in our lives. But from scripture we find that when we come to Him our sin must be dealt with. We cannot stay in His presence without confessing our sins. Acknowledgment will always demand confession.

- Look up Psalm 90:8

Where are our sins, our iniquities?

_____

_____

Would you agree from reading these scriptures that our sins are revealed before Him?

_____

_____

- Read verses 9-10 in Luke chapter 5 and note what Jesus response was to Peter's confession.

Jesus said to Simon, "_____ _____ _____,

from now on you will be _____ _____."

Jesus told Simon that he would no longer be catching fish but that he would be catching men. His life's work would be building the kingdom of God. His life would be different because of his acknowledgment of Jesus' Lordship and the confession of his sin.

ẞENEFIT

A LIFE FOREVER CHANGED

- Turn in your Bible to Romans 10:9-11.

What is the result of belief in Jesus Christ:

_____

What is the result of confession:

_____

Belief with confession always brings about change. A life cannot and will not remain the same when it has put full faith in Jesus Christ and when it has confessed Him as Lord and savior. Many times we find people who are willing to admit that they believe in Jesus but too little do we find those who have confessed or acknowledged Him as their Lord. Not just confessing that He is Lord but asking the question is He My Lord? Have I fallen at His feet confessing my sinfulness and acknowledging Him as my personal Lord and Savior? This is the life-changing question that God is asking to the heart of every woman who is reading this study. This Lordship encounter that Peter had is an encounter that is meant for all of us. Is it any wonder that Peter penned the words to us that God desires for all to be saved and that none perish (II Peter 3:9)? Peter knew this from personal experience.

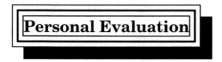

Personal Evaluation

- Has there ever been a time in your life when you have fallen in absolute humility before the Lord and confess your sinfulness, your unworthiness to even be in His presence?

If you have, write a brief description out describing this time in your life: What were the events that God used to bring to this place of confession.

My Place of Confession

_____

_____

_____

_____

_____

Have you ever confessed Jesus as Lord in your own life? A time when you bowed the knee a cried out "Lord, My Lord"?

Salvation is more than believing in Jesus. It's confession of our sinfulness and acknowledging Him as Lord. These are truths that God will change lives with if they will embrace them. I pray that you will search your heart before the throne of God in the light of the truths we have learned so far this week.

I will see you on day four precious student.

We saw on day three of our study this week that Peter saw Jesus and acknowledged Him as his personal Lord and Savior. Peter had witnessed many things about Jesus before this day in the boat, but Peter had never acknowledged Jesus as Lord, and Peter had never confessed his unworthiness.

Let's start today by reading through our passage of study in Luke Chapter 5. Once you've finished I want you to finish writing out verse 11 in the space provided below.

"When they had brought their boats to land, _____ _____ _____ ____ _____ _____."

We find that Peter and the others left everything and followed Jesus from that day forward. Turn to your Word Windows section and look up the meaning for the word **left** and write it out in the space provided below.

Left (KJV-forsook) _____
_____
_____
_____

This word gives us the picture that letting go or giving up something is involved in the action of this word. In meaning; it's a costly following or a costly forsaking.

- Just from looking at verse 11 what did Peter and the others have to give up or leave behind to follow Jesus?

_____

We know they had to leave their boats don't we? This verse tells us that when they had brought their boats back they left all and followed Him. They had to leave their old way of life behind. They were not fishermen anymore for Jesus had given them a new calling, a new purpose for living.

Turn back to your word windows section and look up the word for **followed** and write in the space proved.

Followed _____

_____

_____

_____

This word is very powerful! When Peter and the others forsook everything to follow Jesus they were at that moment joining themselves with Him in likeness and in purpose. This further shows us that a life that follows Jesus will be like Him!

From the day Peter first saw Jesus for who He truly was and confessed it, Peter would be forever drawn to Jesus. We see this over and over again in the life of Peter. A heart that was captivated by Jesus' presence.

Look at these with me and note what you learn from the following verses about Peter's desperation to have and to be with Jesus.

- Matt 14:23-32

_____

_____

_____

_____

- John 13:1-9 (this is the one time that we see Jesus at the feet of man)

_____

_____

- John 13: 31-37

_____

_____

_____

- John 18:1-15

_____

_____

_____

_____

Do you see the drawing power that Jesus has in a life that has come to know Him as Lord? The life that has bowed at the feet of Jesus in full surrender will forever be drawn to Him. Our life's course is changed the moment we surrender, that moment when we fall at His feet and cry "Lord Oh Lord". Jesus was not just Lord that day on the shores of Galilee but He became Peter's Lord. Peter came to know Jesus as his personal Lord and Savior. This is the difference in believing about Jesus and believing in Jesus. And here we see our principle of truth.

YOU CANNOT FOLLOW WHOM YOU HAVE NOT SURRENDERED TO.

If you have never surrendered to the Lordship of Jesus Christ then you cannot be a follower of Jesus Christ. Following involves surrendering, for where there is no surrender there is no following. It's in that moment when one is found in absolute abandonment at the feet of Jesus that a new life is birthed in that sweet hour of surrender and the world will never be the same because of it. How precious it must have been for God to watch as Peter brought that once empty boat, now overflowing with fish, back to the shores that day and leave it there. To see this man and the others walk away from the only life they had ever known to follow His beloved Son. And the world, my precious Bible student, was never the same.

A changed life will mean a changed world for this is God's purpose.

BENEFIT

A NEW PURPOSE FOR LIVING

Peter was a fisherman by trade and had been all of his life, probably like his father before him. He was probably content with fishing, for it was a decent living when the fish were biting. But God had a different plan for Peter's life. Could Peter have possibly known that day he would never be the same? Could he have dared to dream of a new life, a new purpose for rising up every day? Could he have believed that one man would have the power to change his life forever?

Personal Evaluation

- Have you surrendered to the Lord's call, to His will and purpose for your life?

_____

_____

- Have you forsaken all to follow Him? To be identified with Him in likeness, in unity and purpose? Or are there things in your life that are hindering you from following the Lord fully?

_____

_____

In closing, let's review the Principles and Benefits we've learned this week.

Week In Review

Principle	Benefit
We cannot know our emptiness until we see His fullness.	Life overflowing
We cannot acknowledge His Lordship until we acknowledge our sinfulness.	A changed life.
You cannot follow whom you have not surrendered to.	A new purpose for living.

Oh the deep work God wants to do in our hearts, and in our lives. He does not want us to live ordinary lives but rather extraordinary lives full of His glory of demonstrating His power of love to a lost and dying world. I pray that you will take time to meditate upon these Bible truths we have learned from the life of Peter, these are life-giving truths!

Review the memory verse for this week and share it with at least one person. I am so proud of you. Thank you for working so diligently, God will change your life through the study of His Word. I am praying for you. See you in our lesson time together.

May I invite you to have a seat at the feet of Jesus and may you linger there for a while.

<u>NOTES</u>

Luke 5:1-11

1. Now it happened that while the crowd was pressing around Him and listening to the word of God, He was standing by the lake of Gennesaret;

2. and he saw two boats lying at the edge of the lake; but the fishermen had gotten out of them and were washing their nets.

3. And He got into one of the boats, which was Simon's, and asked him to put out a little way from the land. And He sat down and began teaching the people from the boat.

4. When He had finished speaking, he said to Simon, "Put out into the deep water and let down your nets for a catch."

5. Simon answered and said, "Master, we worked hard all night and caught nothing, but I will do as you say and let down the nets."

6. When they had done this, they enclosed a great quantity of fish, and their nets began to break;

7. So they signaled to their partners in the other boat for them to come and help them. And they came and filled both of the boats, so that they began to sink.

8. But when Simon Peter saw that, he fell down at Jesus' feet saying, "Go away from me Lord, for I am a sinful man. O Lord!

9. For amazement had seized him and all his companions because of the catch of fish which they had taken;

10. And so also were James and John, sons of Zebedee, who were partners with Simon. And Jesus said to Simon, "Do not fear, from now on you will be catching men."

11. When they had brought their boats to land, they left everything and followed Him.

The Power of Deliverance

As I am writing this course, the worse natural disaster in American history has just occurred along the eastern coastlines bringing devastation to parts of Louisiana & Mississippi. Many homes and businesses have been flooded and completely swept away. At this hour thousands are missing, thousands have lost their homes, they are without food and clothing, and many have lost everything. Whole cities are underwater with no sign of the waters residing. Stories of great losses continue to come out in the media and some are more than we can bear to watch or listen to. There is anarchy in the streets and martial law has been declared in some places. There are many others this hour, all over the world that are suffering from sickness, disease, poverty, starvation and war. When we see things like these one wonders where is God? Why would God allow such catastrophic events such as 9-11, Hurricane Katrina, the Tsunami, and why would He allow things such as cancer, AIDS, starvation, mental illnesses, homelessness and poverty into the lives of people? All of these are valid questions aren't they?

God is the great physician. He is creator God, El Elyon, the Lord Most High. He is all-powerful, all knowing and He is Holy. He has always been and will forever be. There is nothing God cannot do. God is love yet He is a God of war. He is just and righteous in all His ways yet He is merciful and full of grace. God hates sin, yet He is forgiving and longsuffering wishing for none to perish but for all to have eternal life. God loves us, yet bad things happen everyday all around us. The wonder of God is an

78

awesome, thought provoking, soul-searching act. Who can explain Him?

But we can come to know Him even if we may not understand fully, which we will not until we reach our Heavenly home and our finite minds are supernaturally transformed. I do know that there is but one place to run when tragedies strike, when sickness and difficulties confront us. This place is found only at the feet of Jesus. This is the place where we are to run to, the place we are to fall at in complete surrender and awe. Even when we do not understand, we are to run to His feet not for understanding but for Him and Him alone, and it's in the running that we find He is all that we need. It's in the running precious one, that answers are no longer needed but rather only more of Him.

This week our lesson will be a journey that will reveal great tragedy and show great triumph. We will see the sick healed and the oppressed set free. Let's begin on our knees at the feet of our Savior. Pray and ask Him to transform your mind, conform your will, and inform your spirit. When you are finished come back here and we will begin.

Our study this week will not be centered on one main portion of scripture but rather several that all have the same similarities. The first portion we will look at is found in **Luke chapter 8**. Take a moment and open your Bible and read the entire chapter of Luke 8. This is so important in understanding the context of the scriptures we will look at more closely.

Once you've finished reading the entire chapter, turn to the back of this week's lesson and find the section marked **Luke 8: 26-39.** This is the story of the demonic man. The first thing I want you to do after you've familiarized yourself with this story is go through and highlight every reference to the demonic man in yellow. Make sure you get all the pronouns that refer to him as well.

- Go back to the text and look at every place you highlighted any reference to the demonic man. Make a list below that describes what this man was like when Jesus met him. (An example of the first couple of things you see is: he was from the city, he was possessed with demons, vs. 27)

<u>Demonic Man</u>

This same encounter is recorded in two other places in scripture. They are **Mark 5:2-20** and **Matthew 8:28-34** and they are also typed out for you in the back of this week's lesson. Take a moment and read these two passages and then highlight every reference to the demonic man in the same way you did in Luke chapter 8. In Matthew's encounter you will find that there were two demonic men. Don't let this confuse you. The encounter is centered on the one man in the other two Gospels and that's what we will do as well. Once you've finished marking these two passages, record anything else you learn about this man on your chart.

- What affect did these demons have on the life of this man?

_____

_____

_____

- Was this man a productive person of society?

_____

- What affect did this demonic man's life have on the lives of those who encountered him?

_____

_____

_____

Luke and Matthew described this man as being possessed with demons and Mark described him as one with an unclean spirit. So we know that this man was possessed by demons and these demons are unclean spirits. This is a situation that most of us can't even begin to fathom the reality of. It is something that most have never or will ever witness in their lifetime, yet it was a very real encounter and it is something that is very real even today. Demons are very real and they are very active. This very hour there are people in our world who are held under bondage by demonic or unclean spirits. Most of us would say; "but Pam that only happens in movies, it doesn't happen in real life". Yet God's Word tells us it does.

Every time I read the account of this demonic man my heart is sorrowful for the state this man lived in until he met Jesus. We see from our readings that this man was living among the dead and not among the living. He was in bondage and he had no control over any part of his life, driven by the power of the demons even out into the desert. He was driven to hurt himself; he had no life and no freedom. He had even been unclothed for a long period of time. He was shackled by darkness until he came face to face with the Light Himself. Let's look further now and see what happened when He met Jesus and how did his life change.

• According to Luke 8:28 what was the first thing the man did when he saw Jesus?

_____

_____

• The demonic man cried out in a loud voice when he fell at the feet of Jesus. What did he say? Write it out word for word in the space provided below.

"Seeing Jesus, he cried out and fell before Him, and said in a loud voice",

_____

_____

_____

• What title did the man give Jesus when he addressed Him?

_____

- What title did the man give God?

This man referred to God as "The Most High God" or El Elyon. El Elyon is the name for God that means "Most High". It is the name that designates God as the sovereign ruler of the entire universe. It is one thing to know that God created the heavens and the earth and all that is within them but it's another to know that He is also the one who sustains His creation, fulfilling His purposes for His creation. He made life but He is also wise enough and powerful enough to touch individuals in the everyday moments of their lives. He is the One who rules over all, the One who sits on the throne!

In the light of great tragedies people often struggle with the concept that God is sovereign. But scripture tells us that God is in complete control. He may not be pleased with the things that happen but He is in complete control. Look up and read the following scriptures and write down what you learn about the sovereignty of God.

- Isaiah 14:24 & 27:

- Isaiah 46:9-11

This man, these demons recognized the One Who was over everything. This was a man that could not be controlled even with bonds and fetters. A man who was unclothed, untamed and destructive to himself and to others that came near him. He was a man living in torment every day. Think about this man's life up to the point that Jesus came into his city.

Why do you think this man fell at the feet of Jesus?

_____

_____

To help you better understand how to answer this question let's look in our Word Windows Section for the word **"Seeing"** or in the KJV is "Saw". Once you've located it write its definition in the space provided for you.

Seeing (KJV-saw) _____

_____

_____

_____

_____

In the light of this meaning, why do you think this man fell at the feet of Jesus?

_____

_____

_____

_____

I believe this man recognized, knew, saw who Jesus was, and in seeing Him he fell to his knees in absolute submission. If one has never fallen at the feet of Jesus it is because they have never seen Him for who He really is. He is the Son of the Most High God.

SEEING JESUS FOR WHO HE IS WILL DRIVE YOU TO YOUR KNEES.

This is why we must be diligent to know Jesus. To study His Word, to come to see Him more and more and in seeing Him for who He truly is you, will find yourself bowed low before Him. And as His fullness fills your heart and soul you too will fall on your knees at His feet acknowledging who He is. You will not bow the knee before someone you do not know and you will not submit to one that you do not respect. You might be saying to yourself right now; "Pam, I don't have the desire like I should to be in His Word, or to sit at His feet in prayer and worship". I would ask you a simple question:

- Who do you think Jesus is? What is your perception of Him?

_____

_____

- Read I John 3:2-3
What happens to us when we see Jesus as He is?

_____

I encourage you to get to know Him. This is a life long journey and won't reach its fullness until we step onto the shores of glory and see Him face to face. But as you get to know Him more and more you will find yourself seeking Him more and more and spending time at His feet more and more.

85

- I want to ask you a soul-searching question. Where & how do people see Jesus today?

_____

_____

_____

We know that Jesus isn't going to come walking into our town and so we will not see Him literally in bodily form with our eyes here on this earth as it is now. So how are people going to see Him? Jesus told His disciples, "If you've seen Me, you've seen the Father", meaning that He was a perfect representation of God. Looking at Him was the same as looking at God Himself for Jesus was the God man. Fully God yet fully man. Difficult truth to grasp isn't it? Yet God's Word tells us that Jesus was God (John 1:1 & 14).

Just as Jesus, the Son of God, was a reflection of the Father, so we as His sons and daughters are a reflection of Him also. If we are in Him, He is in us. When people look at us they should see Jesus! When people do see Jesus for who He really is they will fall at His feet. It is at this place of recognition that something wonderful is found. A benefit that will save, deliver, and restore.

BENEFIT

THE PLACE OF SUBMISSION IS FOUND

When the demonic man fell at the feet of Jesus, he found himself in a new place, the place of submission. It is in this place of submission that sweet freedom is found for the soul that is in bondage. Deliverance comes through submission. Many times we want deliverance first before we are willing to submit. But deliverance is the fruit of

submission. You will never find deliverance apart from
submission.

Personal Evaluation

- When people look at you do they see Jesus?

_____

Why or why not?

_____

_____

_____

- Have you ever seen Jesus for who He is?

_____

_____

- Have you looked full in His wonderful face?

_____

_____

Conclusion: Seer this truth upon your heart
precious one:

*Knowing Jesus, seeing Him for who He is, will
keep you at His feet and it will keep you out of
bondage.*

We are on our way to a wonderful study this week! It's been such a blessing to me even as I have written this. Thank you for working so diligently. Press on and don't take shortcuts. Truth takes time. Spiritual insight comes through meditation and prayer. So meditate upon the truths we have seen so far. I will see you on day two precious student.

Welcome back! Let's jump right in, okay? Pray before you begin your study if you haven't already. Read through our text of study in Luke 8 to refresh your memory.

- Go back through our verses of study in Luke, Matthew and Mark that is typed out for you at the end of this lesson and mark every reference to Jesus with a red cross. Once you've finished note what you learned about Jesus and His dealings with this man.

_____

_____

_____

- Did Jesus pass by this man? _____

- What was the first thing we are told that Jesus did? _____

- Did Jesus speak to the man first of did He speak to the unclean spirit?

_____

_____

Did you notice that Jesus addressed the demons first not the man? Jesus first concern was to address that which had the man bound, that which had him in bondage. Jesus' intent was to free this man that he may have life.

- Go back through all three of our passages of study (Luke, Matthew & Mark) once more and underline every reference to the demons. The words change from singular pronouns to plural in the passage when it changes from the man to the unclean spirits, so make sure you pay close attention to the changing of the pronouns so you won't miss anything. Write out below what you learned about these unclean spirits.

_____

_____

Turn to your Word Windows Section in the back of your book and find the word "possess" and record its meaning below.

Possess _____

_____

_____

_____

_____

Isn't it interesting when you look into this Word Window that you see the word possessed comes from the same root word that means to distribute fortunes and or demon? What should this tell us about fortune-tellers and horoscopes? From this word window would you say that someone or something that distributes fortunes is from a good spirit or a bad spirit?

_____

_____

- Jesus asked the man what his name was. What did he tell Jesus his name was?

  _____

- What do the scriptures tell us that the word Legion means?

  _____

- In verse 31 of Luke Chapter 8, what were the demons saying to Jesus?

_____

_____

- In this scene we see that no one up to this point had been able to control this man. When Jesus encounters him who is in control?

_____

- Just from the conversation the demons had with Jesus, who was the one that was in the position of authority?

_____

_____

Just in case you missed it let's look at the word "imploring" (or in the KJV it's "besought") in verse 31. Turn to your Word Windows Section and look up the word imploring.

Imploring (KJV-Besought) _____

_____

_____

_____

Let's look at some other passages of scripture that involve demonic encounters. Read each one and list what you learn beside each verse. There are quite a few so hang on!

- Luke 8:1-2

_____

_____

- Luke 7:21

_____

_____

- Luke 9:1

_____

_____

- Luke 10:17-20

_____

_____

- Luke 9:39-43

_____

_____

- Luke 11:20-26

_____

_____

_____

_____

- Mark 1:32-39

_____

_____

_____

_____

- Mark 7:25-29

_____

_____

From these verses that we have looked at who would you say is the one who has authority over demons, over the spirit world?

_____

As this course is being written there is a movie that has just come out in the movie theaters called" The Exorcism of Emily Rose". This is a movie based on a true story of a girl who was possessed by six demons and who eventually dies. She was never set free from the demons that tormented her life. This movie has sparked a lot of interest as well as, controversy among Churches and those outside the Church. Are demons real? Can they possess people and cause them to act crazy? Can people be delivered from them? The answer to all of these is yes! But if I were to ask you how they are delivered and why they are delivered what would you say? Go back to this encounter with the demonic man that we have been studying about in Luke, Matthew and Mark and you will find the answer.

Everyone can be freed the same way that this man was. What a powerful, freeing truth we find buried here in this account.

Hang on: Are you ready for this?

EVERY SPIRIT MUST BOW IN SUBMISSION TO JESUS CHRIST.

- Look up Ephesians 1:18-23: According to this passage who is above all?

_____

What does this truth mean to us who bow the knee to Him? It means freedom precious friend. It means that the day the captive bows the knee of authority in submission to the Lord Jesus Christ and cries out to Him from his whole being he will be set free! The spirit of fear must bow, every enemy of God, every spirit clean or unclean must and will bow in submission to Jesus when confronted by Him.

There are thousands of people in our world even this hour that are held in the grip of demonic forces. There are thousands in mental institutions suffering because our medical world, as advanced as it is, cannot help them because they cannot cure them. I do believe there are physical conditions that make us sick but I also believe according to God's Word that there are spiritual conditions that make us sick physically, and mentally.
What is the answer? We've seen it this week in God's Word precious one! We know that every spirit must bow the knee in the presence of Jesus! Because this is true the life transforming benefit is:

ℬENEFIT

THE CAPTIVE IS FREE

Are you living in bondage? Do you know someone who is? Bondage comes in many different forms from drugs and alcohol to relationships; fear, depression, eating disorders, finances and pornography just to name a few. Do you remember our study of Isaiah 61:1 from last week? Remember that Jesus read this scripture and said that it had been fulfilled in their presence. Jesus was talking about Himself. Look with me again at these powerful words.

"The Spirit of the Lord is upon me, because he anointed Me to preach the Gospel to the poor. He has sent Me to proclaim release to the captives, and recovery of sight to the blind, to set free those who are oppressed. To proclaim the favorable year of the Lord."

- Out of this passage which of these did Jesus do for this demon possessed man?

_____

_____

There are many things that enslave us, many things that hold us captive and rob us of a life of freedom. Based on our study this week, do you think that anyone can be freed from bondage, even those who are demon possessed?

_____

_____

If yes, how are they freed?

_____

Is there anything in your life that you are in bondage too? If so list it out below.

_____

_____

_____

Based on God's Word that you have studied so far this week, how can you be freed from the bondage?

_____

What must you do to be free?

_____

_____

I want to leave you with our memory verse for this week; Galatians 5:1. I have typed it out for you below. Memorize it that it may be stored in your heart forever!

It was for freedom that Christ has set us free; therefore keep standing firm and do not be subject again to a yoke of slavery.

You have worked so very hard today. I know this lesson was a long one but well worth the work! These truths that you are learning and will continue to learn are so vital and so important to understand and believe in especially in the day and time we are living in. There are many suffering, held in bondage, captive, living among the dead, isolated from the rest of society, tormented day and night because they have not seen Jesus. They have not fallen at the feet of the very one who can release them. The one who can restore them to the land of the living. Demonic activity is very real in our world and the problem is that we don't know how to help those who are afflicted by them.

Thank you so much for your diligent study. I am praying for you precious friend. I will see you on day three.

What a wonderful week we've had so far! We have learned that there is power in seeing Jesus and bowing before Him in submission. We have also learned that every spirit must bow the knee before the Lord Jesus Christ and in the bowing the captive is set free! Halleluiah! Today we are going to dive a little deeper and see more life giving truths from the demonic man when he encountered Jesus. Don't forget to pray and ask God to open the eyes of your understanding that you may behold wonderful truths from His word.

Begin by reading through our main passage of study this week found in Luke 8 typed out in the back of this lesson. Once you've read through it to refresh your memory, I want you to write out what the demons said to Jesus in verse 28 of Luke. Write it out word for word in the space provided. I have started it for you.

Seeing Jesus, he cried out and fell before Him, and said in a loud voice, _____

_____

_____

What do you think the man meant when he said "what business do we have with each other? The King James Version says; *"what do I have to do with you"*.

_____

_____

The Amplified Bible expounds this verse to read; *"what do we have in common"*. I want you to look up a verse that will help you to understand what was meant by this question. Once you've read it write out any insight that it gives you.

- II Corinthians 6:14

_____

Look up the following verses and write out what you learn about light and darkness from each.
- John 1:1-9

_____

_____

- John 3:16-21

_____

_____

- John 8:12

_____

_____

- I John 1:5-6

_____

_____

Read Acts 26:12-18. The apostle Paul is speaking in these verses and is testifying to his salvation. Take note of what you learn about light and darkness.

_____

_____

_____

In view of these verses we've just read about "the Light" what do you think the man meant when he said to Jesus; "what do we have to do with each other"?

_____

_____

_____

I believe it's the same principle as clean and unclean; that they do not have anything in common with one another. These demons knew who Jesus was and they knew that they did not belong in His presence. How could they belong in His presence? They were unclean and He was the Holy Son of God. Darkness and light have nothing in common. Let's look further at the conversation that the unclean spirits had with Jesus.

What was the first thing that Jesus said to the unclean spirits? See if you can find it on your own and write it out below.

_____

Jesus immediately commanded the unclean spirit to come out of the man. What was the response?

_____

_____

What request did the demons make of Jesus?

_____

What did they ask Him not to do?

_____

Go back to the other two passages found in Mark and Matthew and re-read through this story once again. Highlight everything that the demons actually said to Jesus. Once you've finished, record everything you learned from marking in the space provided.

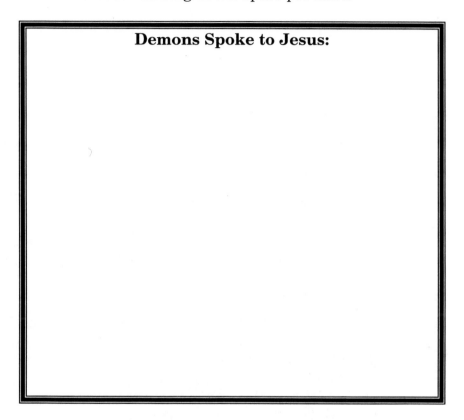

Demons Spoke to Jesus:

Did you note that the demons asked Jesus did He come to torment them before it was time? We saw that the demons also requested that Jesus not send them away to the abyss or the bottomless pit.

Look up the following verses and record what you learn about the abyss or bottomless pit. Don't be concerned with trying to understand the prophetic meaning but focus on what you learn about the abyss and what it might be. It will help you to ask; who, what, when, where and how questions. I will help you by telling you that the abyss and bottomless pit are referring to the same place.

- Revelation 9: 1-11

_____

_____

_____

- Revelation 20:1-3

_____

_____

_____

The abyss or bottomless pit was a holding place for the unclean spirits also known as demons. It is here that they are held and cannot escape from unless one who has the key comes and opens it and allows them to be released. I hope you noted also in your reading of these passages that the key is held and controlled by God Himself. Let it be understood that Satan does not hold this key!

Read Hebrews 2:14 and answer the questions below:

Who did Jesus render powerless?

_____

How did Jesus render Satan powerless?

_____

Did Satan have power before Jesus took it from him? If so what power did he have?

_____

What a truth we see emerging from the scriptures!!! This is a truth that has held me steady in the darkest of times. A truth that removes all fear!

PRINCIPLE

DARKNESS CANNOT STAY IN THE PRESENCE OF LIGHT.

Darkness precious child will never overcome the light for the darkness has already been overcome by the Light. It is not a battle yet to be won, it has already been won! We have just seen this truth in Hebrews 2:14. When the darkness left this man something miraculous happened. His life was returned to him. Before he was living in the land of the dead, among the tombs and in the shadows. He was uncontrollable and he often would hurt himself physically. But once the light came all that changed. Read our passage of study again. Where did Jesus send the demons?

_____

What happened to them once they entered the herd of swine?

_____

Do you see it precious friend? Darkness cannot stay in the presence of the Light but the darkness is also utterly destroyed! Praise the Lord. God doesn't intend for us to contend with the darkness forever! The darkness has a day of death coming, amen?!!! You and I cannot only be freed from the darkness but the darkness itself can be utterly destroyed by Jesus.

𝔅ENEFIT

DARKNESS IS DESTROYED

You cannot be a child of God and remain in darkness, for darkness and light have nothing in common. Jesus intends to destroy every area of darkness by bringing it into the light! It's only here that darkness must flee and it is only here that darkness is cast out forever.

Praise the Lord! Jesus' intention was not to just cast out the demons for that moment, or the darkness just for that moment, but He intended to cast them out forever! Never to return again. Jesus gives eternal freedom.

Personal Evaluation

Is there anything in your life that your are opening yourself up to that might lead to something displeasing to God? Why don't you take a moment and fall at the feet of your sweet Savior and ask Him to reveal any areas of bondage, any areas of darkness that is in your life. Revelation comes at His feet and His feet alone, it is found nowhere else! Write out what He speaks to your heart.

Dear Lord,

Do you find yourself isolated from others, living not in the land of the living but finding yourself dwelling in the shadows of death? A land where there is no sign of life, no sign of hope? If so what would you say to yourself at this very moment in the light of this study?

_____

_____

_____

Bondage is anything that keeps you from life. Bondage will only bring you to barren lands. How I am praying for you as I write this course that you will know the power that comes from falling at the feet of Jesus.

You've worked very hard today, thank you so much. Practice your memory verse and write it out below! This will help you memorize scripture..

_____

_____

_____

I will see you on day four!!!

We've come to our last lesson this week and as we close out this marvelous study of the demonic man I want us to soak it all in and see this wonderful ending to this man's story. It's one that stirs my heart every time I read it. How I pray that it stirs your heart as well. Pray before you begin your study.

Turn to our main passages of study in Luke 8 and refresh your memory by reading through it once. When you've finished I want you to meditate on the last few verses of this passage namely verses 33-39. Read through it again and this time I want you to mark every reference to the people who saw the demonic man after Jesus commanded the demons to leave. Choose any color you like and draw a circle around any reference to them. Once you finished go back and note everywhere you marked these references and take note of what you learn. Record your insights below.

Witnesses

- What affect do you think this man's life had on the lives of others before Jesus cast out the demons?

_____

_____

_____

- What affect do you think this man's life had on the lives of others after Jesus cast out the demons?

_____

_____

_____

- Go back and review every place that you marked the demonic man earlier in the week (make sure you look at all three accounts). Answer the following questions:

How did the demons affect the man spiritually?

_____

_____

_____

How did the demons affect the man physically?

_____

_____

_____

How did the demons affect the man emotionally?

_____

_____

_____

These are such vital questions to ask when studying these passages. This man was in bondage and this bondage affected him, spiritually, physically and emotionally. Once this man was freed from his bondage how did his life change? The sign or evidence that deliverance had come was in his changed life. Let's look closely again at these last few verses; 33-39 and take note of how his life changed by comparing before and after. We want to see how this man's life changed when Jesus set him free.

Before   **After**

Spiritual State

Physical State

Emotional State

Do you see the power and affect that bondage has on our lives?

Turn to Luke chapter 8 and write out verse 35 in the space provide for you below:

_____

_____

_____

This man's whole life changed instantaneously! How many times have you seen this in a person's life? It's not every day that we get to witness a demonic man delivered before our very eyes. It's not every day that we get to witness a man go from hurting himself and completely out of control to sitting at the feet of Jesus in His right mind fully clothed. Do you see the power that Jesus had upon this man's life? What an affect that Jesus had on this man's life? But this man's life affected the lives of others in a powerful way!!! Some were afraid, others were filled with awe and wonder, and still others wanted no part of Jesus because of it. When man can't explain it he will usually do one of two things: fear it or want nothing to do with it. What did this man do with Jesus once he met Him? The first time he encountered Jesus we see that he fell at His feet but now what do we see this man doing with Jesus?

_____

_____

When Jesus was leaving how did this man react?

_____

_____

This man never wanted to be separated from Jesus again!
Who could blame him! What did Jesus tell the man to do
now that he was free? Hint look in verse 29. Write it out
word for word in the space provided.

But He sent him away saying,

_____

_____

_____

In your own words describe how this man's deliverance
impacted the world around him?

_____

_____

_____

A changed life is a beautiful thing isn't it? It's also a
powerful tool in the hands of God to impact the lives of
those who witness it. This man once naked was now fully
clothed. This man once in chains was now free from all
shackles. This man once living in the tombs was now in
the land of the living. This man who was gripped by the
power of demonic forces was now held in the grip of Jesus!
This man once a lunatic, shunned by all was now in his
right mind sitting at the feet of a King! God doesn't just
deliver but He fully restores!

PRINCIPLE

FREEDOM BRINGS RESTORATION.

Jesus told the man to return to his home and describe the great things God had done for him. The man did just that. Could you imagine if this man once he was freed from the demons, continued to live in the tombs, unclothed and in shackles? Freedom came when he fell at Jesus' feet, but restoration came when he sat at His feet.

Why did God free us? Why did He free this man? It's true that God wants us to be free and not to live in bondage, but He has more that He wants to do than free us! Can you guess what it is?

What happened to this man once he was freed? Do you remember how people saw him before he was freed? How do the people see him now after he fell at the feet of Jesus? Look in our passages of study and see if you can find the answer.

_____

_____

_____

How amazing this complete transformation was to all who witnessed it. They saw and sat in complete awe and wonder. Freedom brings restoration, but restoration brings forth a powerful testimony.

ℬENEFIT

A POWERFUL TESTIMONY

God delivers so that He may be praised among the people. Often times we are so ashamed of our former lives that we hide our testimony from the rest of the world and God never gets the intended praise. Though we are very thankful for God's deliverance we often keep silent because of fear, worried what others would think of us if we told what we were before Jesus saved us!

Read II Timothy 1:12 and write down what you learned about Paul and what he believed about the Lord.

_____

_____

Paul knew whom He had believed in and was fully convinced that He was able to guard it until the day of eternity. Paul was grateful for his deliverance because he knew from Whom it came and what a powerful testimony he had because of it!

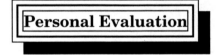

Personal Evaluation

What keeps you from testifying of God's mercy and deliverance in your life?

_____

_____

This man didn't even want to go home, but rather he wanted to sit at the feet of Jesus and he wanted to go with Him when He left. Jesus is the one who told Him to go home. When Jesus delivers you, you will not have a problem following Him! Are you so thankful that Jesus delivered you that you would follow Him no matter where He went? What are others saying about your life?

These are soul-searching questions aren't they? I pray that you will grasp the depth of these truths and you will know the joy of living in the land of freedom and the power found sitting at the feet of Jesus. Let's take a quick review of our week together:

Week In Review

Principle	Benefit
Seeing Jesus for who He really is will drive you to your knees	Place of Submission
Every spirit must bow in Submission to Jesus	The Captive is Freed
Darkness cannot stay in the presence of Light	Darkness Destroyed
Freedom brings Restoration	A Powerful Testimony

Thank you for a wonderful time of study this week. I have prayed for you earnestly that you will be heard saying to the master Himself, "I want to go with you Lord". May others see you and stand in awe and wonder at the power of God.

In closing I want to share these words with you...

I once was bound by shackles, but now I've been set free
The fetters bound so tightly no longer hinder me,
My feet run in freedom, my lips now sing thy praise
For from the tombs of death, my life Your hand did raise
Lost in utter darkness, I cried both day and night
Then at the feet of Jesus, the darkness fled in Light
Don't look for me in barren lands or among the dessert plains
I'm drinking from celestial fountains drawn from Emanuel's veins

Review your memory verse and I will see you in our lesson time together. Love to you precious student....

May I invite you to have a seat at the feet of Jesus and may you linger there for a while.

NOTES

27. And when He came out onto the land, He was met by a man from the city who was possessed with demons; and who had not put on any clothing for a long time, and was not living in a house, but in the tombs.

28. Seeing Jesus, he cried out and fell before Him, and said in a loud voice, "What business do we have with each other, Jesus, Son of the Most High God? I beg you, do not torment me."

29. For He had commanded the unclean spirit to come out of the man. For it had seized him many times; and he was bound with chains and shackles and kept under guard, and yet he would break his bonds and be driven by the demon into the desert.

30. And Jesus asked him, "What is your name?" And he said, "Legion"; for many demons had entered him.

31. They were imploring Him not to command them to go away into the abyss.

32. Now there was a herd of many swine feeding there on the mountain; and the demons implored Him to permit them to enter the swine. And He gave them permission.

33. And the demons came out of the man and entered the swine; and the herd rushed down the steep bank into the lake and was drowned.

34. When the herdsmen saw what had happened, they ran away and reported it in the city and out in the country.

35. The people went out to see what had happened; and they came to Jesus, and found the man from whom the demons had gone out, sitting down at the feet of Jesus, clothed in his right mind; and they became frightened.

36. Those who had seen it reported to them how the man who was demon possessed had been made well.

37. And all the people of the country of the Gerasenes and the surrounding district asked Him to leave them, for they were gripped with fear; and He got into a boat and returned.

38. But the man from whom the demons had gone out was begging Him that he might accompany Him; but He sent him away saying,

39. "Return to your house and describe what great things god has done for you." So he went away, proclaiming throughout the whole city what great things Jesus had done for him.

Mark 5:2-20

2. When He got out of the boat, immediately a man from the tombs with an unclean spirit met Him,

3. And he had his dwelling among the tombs. An no one was able to bind him anymore, even with a chain;

4. Because he had often been bound with shackles and chains, and the chains had been torn apart by him and the shackles broken in pieces, and no one was strong enough to subdue him.

5. Constantly, night and day, he was screaming among the tombs and in the mountains, and gashing himself with stones.

6. Seeing Jesus from a distance, he ran up and bowed down before Him;

7. And shouting with a loud voice, he said, "What business do we have with each other, Jesus, Son of the Most High God? I implore You by God, do not torment me!"

8. For he had been saying to him, "Come out of the man, you unclean spirit!"

9. And He was asking him, "What is your name?" and he said to Him, "My name is Legion; for we are many."

10. And he began to implore Him earnestly not to send them out of the country.

11. Now there was a large herd of swine feeding nearby on the mountain.

12. The demons implored Him saying, "Send us into the swine so that we may enter them."

13. Jesus gave them permission. And coming out, the unclean spirits entered the swine; and the herd rushed down the steep bank into the sea, about two thousand of them; and they were drowned in the sea.

14. Their herdsmen ran away and reported it in the city and in the country. And the people came to see what it was that had happened.

15. They came to Jesus and observed the man who had been demon-possessed sitting down, clothed and in his right mind, the very man who had had the "legion"; and they became frightened.

16. Those who had seen it described to them how it had happened to the demon-possessed man, and all about the swine.

17. And they began to implore Him to leave their region.

18. As He was getting into the boat, the man who had been demon-possessed was imploring Him that he might accompany Him.

19. And He did not let him, but He said to him, "Go home to your people and report to them what great things the Lord has done for you, and how He had mercy on you."

20. And he went away and began to proclaim in Decapolis what great things Jesus had done for him; and everyone was amazed.

28. When He came to the other side into the country of the Gardarenes, two men who were demon-possessed met Him as they were coming out of the tombs. They were so extremely violent that no one could pass by that way.

29. And they cried out, saying, "What business do we have with each other, Son of God? Have you come here to torment us before the time?"

30. Now there was a herd of many swine feeding at a distance from them.

31. The demons began to entreat Him saying, "If you are going to cast us out, send us into the herd of swine?"

32. And He said to them, "Go!" And they came out and went into the swine, and the whole herd rushed down the steep bank into the sea and perished in the waters.

33. The herdsmen ran away, and went to the city and
reported everything, including what had happened
to the demoniacs.

34. And behold, the whole city came out to meet Jesus;
and when they saw Him, they implored Him to
leave their region.

The Grieving Heart

DAY ONE

It was a busy fall morning; there were guests in the house and the day held a flurry of activities at the Church. The young mother rushed to prepare breakfast for her husband, two children and parents who had come up for a visit, before rushing out the door to the Church. She would go on ahead of them and the family was to meet her later at the Church. Little did she know as she rushed out the door that morning that it would be the last time she would see any of them alive. As her husband, two children, and her mother and father were driving to the Church that morning they were struck by a train and killed. It was a great tragedy that fell with full force upon this quiet country town that morning and brought utter devastation to the heart of a young mother. It's unfathomable to most to even begin to take in the depth of grief that this woman must have experienced. This was a strong Christian family that loved the Lord and served Him faithfully in their community and in their Church. When faced with such a sad situation the natural instinct of the heart of man is to ask why God? Why would you allow something so painful? How could any one survive such a tragedy? How could anything good come from this situation? Where was this young woman to run? She was an only child and had little or no family to turn to except her Church family.

This story touched many lives on the deepest level as they grieved with this young woman because of her great loss. Although this story is one of great loss, it is only one of thousands upon thousands that have affected the lives of people all over the world throughout history. It's difficult to find someone whose life hasn't been touched by tragedy in some way. I know of another woman who lost all four of her young sons when they were killed suddenly in a car accident while driving to school one morning. It seems unthinkable doesn't it? Yet these things happen every day all around the world. Some stories too painful to even hear or read about. Grief is very real and it will affect each of us during our lifetime at some point or another.

How do we deal with grief? Where do we run to find comfort, to find peace beyond comprehension? How can we survive the loss of a loved one when they are taken away from us? How can a mother's heart be made whole again when she loses a child? Can the widow's heart ever find her song again once her beloved is gone? Will a broken heart ever be made whole again? This will be our journey this week precious student. We will see the depth of grief and suffering in the lives of God's children and we will see the only place to find joy and strength in the midst of them. Joy can be found; strength and comfort can come to any soul no matter the loss. I hope you are ready. If you've prayed then let's begin.

Our main text of study this week will be John 11: 11-45. It is a story most familiar to many of us; it is the story of the death and resurrection of Lazarus. John is the only gospel that tells us of this powerful event so this is where we will spend the majority of our time of study. The setting is in a small village on the southeastern slopes of the Mount of Olives. It is about two miles east of Jerusalem near the road to Jericho; it is the city of Bethany. A tragedy has come to this small village and it has grieved the heart of many people. Let's begin by reading through this passage, which is typed out in the back of this week's lesson for you.

Now that you have familiarized yourself with the story write out below a brief summary of what happened in these verses. I'm not looking for a lot of detail at this point, just a brief overview of what happened written in your own words.

The story of the death and resurrection of Lazarus

Using a color of your choice I want you to read through this passage again but his time I want you to draw a box around any reference to Lazarus. Once you've finished come back and make a list of every thing you learned about Lazarus by marking his name. For example, the first thing we learn about Lazarus that we could list would be that he was from Bethany.

Lazarus

_____

_____

_____

From what you've learned so far about Lazarus would you say that Jesus cared about him? Does this passage give you any idea how Jesus felt about Lazarus and his family? Explain your answer in the space provided below.

_____

_____

Go back through our passage of study but this time underline every reference to sick or sickness with a color of your choosing. Make it a different color from that of Lazarus so you can differentiate between the two easily when you look at the passage.

In verse 4 of this passage what kind of sickness does Jesus say this is going to be? How is it going to be used, according to Jesus?

_____

_____

To help us get a better view of this situation turn to your Word Windows section in the back of your book and locate the definition for sickness and write it in the space provided.

Sickness_____

_____

_____

_____

We see and understand that Lazarus had an infirmity, a sickness. He was in a state of weakness and was lacking strength. Sounds pretty serious doesn't it?

Did it appear that Jesus was worried or concerned that Lazarus was sick?

_____

_____

From all appearance it seemed that Jesus was not concerned at all when He was told that Lazarus was sick because the scriptures tell us that He waited two days longer before He decided to head over to Bethany. Let's take a deep look at Jesus in this passage.

Go through and mark every reference to Jesus by drawing a red cross over them. Remember this helps Jesus to stand out in the text so when we are observing the text He will be easily seen to us. Once you have finished marking every reference to Jesus come back and make a list of anything you may have learned about Jesus from this passage and from your markings.

Jesus

_____

_____

_____

_____

Do you think that this situation grieved the heart of Jesus? Support your answer.

_____

_____

_____

We know from these verses that Jesus loved Lazarus and we know that He was saddened by his death because Jesus wept at Lazarus tomb. Yet, when we read verse 15 in our passage of study we see something vital that Jesus says to His disciples. Look up verse 15 in your study passage and write this verse out in the space provided.

Was Jesus glad or sad that He wasn't there when Lazarus died?

Why do you think Jesus said this? What do you think He meant by the words; "I'm glad for your sakes that I was not there"?

This was a difficult moment for the family of Lazarus and for the disciples. They were having a very hard time understanding what Jesus was saying to them. We know that Jesus loved Lazarus and his sisters. He was grieved to the point that he wept openly. Yet why did Jesus not go immediately to help Lazarus when He heard that he was sick? Was it that He didn't love him? No, the scriptures tell us that He did love Lazarus. Was it that He had no compassion on their situation? No, the scriptures reveal that Jesus' heart was deeply moved and grieved for this family and their situation.

From what we've studied so far, is it safe to say that Jesus loved them so very much yet He allowed pain to touch their lives even when He had the power to stop it?

_____

It's difficult for most to accept that God allows tragedy into the lives of those whom He loves. Yet God does allow it and He is touched with our grief as well. When we grieve, He grieves with us and over us. But what moves us beyond the grief? What moved Jesus beyond the grief of the moment when He heard the news about Lazarus, the one He loved? Jesus saw beyond the temporal affliction. He saw beyond the circumstance into eternity.

Look at verse 4 once again and write it out below. This is a most powerful verse.
"But when Jesus heard this, He said,_____

_____

_____ "

Look up the word Glory in your Word Windows section and write it out in the space provided. You looked up this word once before in our study but for a review and to help shed light on these verses write it out once more. This is the same word as used previously in lesson two of our study of Peter's fishing encounter with Jesus.

Glory_____
_____
_____
_____

Glory is that which reveals who God is. It is an adequate representation of Him and who He is. God's desire is to reveal Himself to mankind. Jesus wasn't looking at the tragedy of the moment. His focus was not on Lazarus being deathly sick. His concern was not for the sickness, but his attention was upon the purpose of the sickness. Jesus had an eternal perspective on the situation at hand. He knew that there was a greater end coming.

PRINCIPLE

TRAGEDIES SERVE A HIGHER PURPOSE.

We do not suffer in vain! How do we handle the unbearable situations? We look through Heaven's eyes. We look not at the things, which are seen but that which is not seen (II Corinthians 4:18). Take a minute and look up this verse in your Bible and write it out below. This will be your memory verse this week precious student.

- II Corinthians 4:18

_____

_____

_____

This will be a powerful verse to have stored in your heart. It will hold you even in times of greatest difficulty. Memorize it well. Jesus Himself applied this truth to His own life when He faced the agony of Calvary's death. Look up Hebrews 12:2. How was Jesus able to endure death?

_____

What was Jesus focused on?

_____

Aren't you glad that sufferings have a purpose, that they have meaning? Sufferings are put into a whole new perspective, aren't they?

What did Jesus say to Martha in verse 40 of John Chapter 11?

"Jesus said to her,_____

_____

_____?"

Jesus clearly reveals the benefit of this powerful principle in this verse.

BENEFIT

A GREATER GLORY IS REVEALED

Jesus was looking toward the greater glory. He was looking beyond the temporal and into eternity. You see Jesus knew what the outcome was going to be. He knew that ultimately in the end joy would be restored and God would be glorified in a way that He could not have if the circumstances had been different. The difficulty lies in whether or not we desire the greater glory and whether or not we believe God when He says that it will be for the greater glory. How often have we prayed to God, "I pray that you would get the glory"? But do we realize what we are really praying? God's glory could mean our suffering and many times it does. Moses prayed this prayer with great earnestness and desperation. Take a moment and read the verse below.

• Exodus 33:18

What was Moses' prayer to God in this verse?

_____

_____

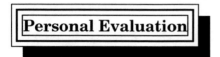

Personal Evaluation

Is your heart's desire to see God's glory displayed?

Do you trust Him for the end result?

Are there tragedies that have happened in your life or in your family's life that you have had a difficult time accepting? If so how do you think God would want you to respond?

_____

_____

We may not understand them but God has a greater purpose in even the most tragic of circumstances. We seek to understand the "why" or we fill our thoughts with the "what ifs" and when this happens we will not only live in constant sorrow we will never look beyond that which is seen and we will miss the precious glimpse of the "unseen". It's the unseen that brings comfort and the need for understanding fades away in the presence of it. God looks beyond the temporal, for that's what sufferings are, they are only temporal. Aren't you glad precious one? One day all of our sorrows are going to flood away as a forgotten wave upon the shores of our lives. Every tear will be wiped away by the very hand of Jesus Himself. The glory of God is beautiful even in sadness if we will but look through Heaven's eyes.

I pray that you will look not at the things that you can see, but that which you cannot see. You've been diligent in our lesson today and I'm so proud of you. You are learning precious truths that will never leave you. I will see you on day two precious student.

DAY TWO

Yesterday we began to get a glimpse of how to deal with tragedies, or difficult situations. Grief is very real and it is not a respecter of persons for all of us are touched by it in our lifetime, some more than others. Turn to John 11 and read through our passage of study one time through just to refresh your memory. Pray before you begin asking God to open the eyes of your understanding that you may behold wonderful things from His Word. God's Word says you shall know the truth and the truth shall set you free.

We looked at Lazarus and Jesus primarily on day one. Today we're going to continue our study by marking every reference to Martha and Mary. Remember Lesson One? We've already studied these two sisters earlier. Let's draw a circle around each one using two different colors so we can differentiate between the two easily when we make our lists in a moment. For example, you might want to draw a pink circle around every reference to Mary and a Yellow circle around every reference to Martha. This is only a suggestion! Choose any color that you haven't already used in this week's lesson so far. Start with Martha first and then Mary second.

Make a list of anything you learned about Martha.

Martha

136

Make a list of anything you learned about Mary.

Mary

Did you see any difference between these two sisters in the way they handled this situation?

_____

_____

_____

Let me ask you a couple of questions:

When we first studied Mary and Martha in lesson one of this study, what did we see Martha doing? (Turn back to lesson one if you need to review)

_____

What did we first see Mary doing?

_____

In this scene we are studying in John 11, what do we see Martha doing when she sees Jesus?

What do we see Mary doing when she sees Jesus?

Both sisters said the same thing to Jesus but their actions toward Him were completely different. Martha began speaking to Jesus but the scriptures tell us that Mary fell out His feet weeping when she began to speak. Do you see a difference in the way these two women handled there grief? Martha met Jesus but Mary hurried (or ran) to Jesus. Martha did not fall at His feet, Mary did. The first time we see Mary she is sitting at Jesus' feet and now this time we see her falling at His feet. I believe there are times when we sit at His feet, but there are times when we fall at His feet. In our times of grief, in our times when the pain is unbearable, this is the time to fall at His feet. There is no safer ground to fall upon than that, which is before His nail pierced feet. You see, to Mary this was a familiar place for her, for she had been there before at His feet. This was the only place she knew to run, she need not run elsewhere for He was her everything, her very life. When you sit at His feet in the midst of peace you will fall at His feet in the midst of the storms.

I want us to look at the heart of Jesus as He encountered Mary and the others when He arrived in Bethany. Take a colored pencil or highlighter of your choice and reading through verses 30-38 of John chapter 11, I want you to highlight or color every reference to: wept or weeping, the phrase, "deeply moved", and the word troubled.

138

From what you've marked how did this affect Jesus personally?

_____

_____

Would you say that this situation grieved the heart of Jesus or did it even bother Him at all?

_____

_____

Turn to your Word Windows section and look up the following words and record their meanings beside each:

Deeply (KJV-groaned)_____

_____

_____

_____

Troubled_____

_____

_____

Wept_____

_____

_____

Based upon the meanings of the words write out in your own words how you think Jesus must have felt?

_____

_____

Even though Jesus waited before He went to Lazarus would you say that Jesus cared based upon what you've learned so far?

_____

There are only two times in the life of Christ that we know that He cried. The first is here at the tomb of Lazarus and the second is in the garden of Gethsemane when He was facing His own death.

Do you think there has ever been a time when Jesus wept over you? If so, write it out.

_____

_____

Look up the following verses and note what you learned from each:

- I Peter 5:6-7

_____

_____

- Psalm 55:22

_____

_____

- Psalm 56:9-10

_____

_____

PRINCIPLE

JESUS CARES FOR ME.

Jesus doesn't just care in general, He cares about you personally. Do you remember the words of Martha when she approached Jesus with her complaint when Jesus was in her home? She said; "do you not care Lord"? To know and believe that Jesus really does care for me even when bad things happen will bring comfort that the arm of the flesh can never give to us. The first thing one should remind themselves of when faced with difficult situations is: "God cares for me". God never stops caring for His children.

The moment we embrace this truth God/Jesus becomes personal to us. Because the Lord cares for me what should this mean and what does this mean to my life? How should this affect my everyday life?

Let's look at a verse that I think will help us answer these questions.

• Psalm 144:1-2
Once you have read this fill in the blanks according to this scripture.

Vs. 1 *The Lord is my* _____

Vs. 2 *The Lord is my* _____ *and my* _____

The Lord is my _____ *and my* _____

My _____ *and He in whom I* _____ _____

This is an awesome verse isn't it? To know in the deepest part of your soul that God is your rock, He is your loving-kindness, He is your fortress, He is your stronghold, He is your deliverer, He is your shield and He is the one you can take refuge in. Do you know why Mary fell at Jesus feet? She fell at His feet because she knew all this about Him. Jesus was her rock and her fortress and He was her security. Jesus was her stronghold and she needed to be held strongly. Jesus was the only one who could deliver her and protect her and her family and so in knowing this, she fell before Him because He was her only hope.

Grief cannot come near when you are in the presence of Joy. Fear cannot overwhelm you when you are in a strong and mighty fortress. He will protect you and cover you with His pinions for He is a shield about you. Mary knew this in the deepest part of her being.

- Read II Corinthians 1: 3-4
According to these verses where is comfort found?

_____

Turn to your Word Windows Section and find the meaning of the word Comfort and record it below.

Comfort (KJV-comforteth) _____

_____
_____
_____

If I take this rich word meaning, precious student and apply it to this verse we see that, God is the God who draws near to us, coming along side of us to give aide in our time of need. In times of grief invite God to draw near to you! Knowing this truth let me ask you a question.

Can God comfort us in any situation no matter how tragic?

_____

What a mighty truth Mary knew that Jesus cared and because He cared for her she had a source of comfort.

ℬENEFIT

A PLACE OF COMFORT IS FOUND

Do you remember Jesus very words on the Sermon on the Mount?
Look up Matthew 5:4 and write this verse out below.

How can we be blessed or happy as it can be translated, when we mourn? Because we have a source of comfort and it's found in Jesus because He cares for us. You may be a woman who would say to me: "Pam, my heart will never know joy again, because my sorrow is too deep". I understand there are sorrows beyond words. Sorrows so deep that they crush the heart seemingly beyond repair. I've held many a woman in my arms that have trod the valley of deep sorrow. I have also walked through that valley so I know the groanings of a broken heart. But did I know joy again! Yes! Oh that I could take you to the feet of Jesus precious student. You can know joy again for He turns sorrow into to gladness. Isaiah 51:11 says in speaking of the Lord's coming that…"*sorrow and sighing will flee away*". Why would sorrow and sighing flee away? It's because the Lord was coming! There is but one place that sorrow will flee from and that's in the presence of Jesus.

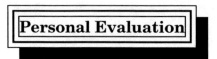

Mary was surrounded by others who sought to comfort her but yet she was not comforted until Jesus came. The arm of the flesh will never give you what only Jesus can. Yes we can hold one another and comfort as best as humanly possible, but the comfort found in the Lord goes much deeper than a physical touch ever will. His comfort goes straight to the heart and soul.

Is there grief in your life that you have not taken to the feet of Jesus?

_____

_____

Is your life filled with constant sorrow? What would the Lord have you to do at this very moment?

_____

_____

Do you know and firmly believe that God does care about you and that He is the God of all comfort? Explain why or why not.

_____

_____

"When you can't find God in your difficulties, you'll discover Him in your praise"

Dr. David Jeremiah

Why don't you take just a moment and write out a prayer to the Lord praising Him for Who He is and what He means to your life thanking Him that He does care and comfort you.

Dear Lord,

_____

_____

_____

_____

_____

_____

Let's close today by reviewing our memory verse. Thank you for your diligent study. What a good student you are! I'm praying for you dear friend, hang in there and don't quit till we have finished our course!

Welcome back precious student. Well so far this week we have learned from our study of God's Word in John Chapter 11 that tragedies serve a higher purpose. Tragedies don't just randomly happen; they are according to God's plan and God's timing. They are all serving His purpose, which is always to bring glory to His Holy name. We also learned that Jesus does care even when bad things happen and because He cares for us we can find in Him all that we need in any situation. Today I want us to look at the people who were watching in the midst of Lazarus death and resurrection. We know how this tragedy affected Mary and Martha and we know how it affected Jesus Himself, but how did it affect the lives of the people who witnessed it? It's going to be a wonderful study for us today! Take a minute and pray before you begin.

Let's begin our study by reading verses 32-45 of John Chapter 11. Once you've read through it go back a second time and taking a color you haven't used yet in this lesson underline every reference to the Jews who were watching and to any reference made to the Pharisees. Remember to get your pronouns such as them or they. Record what you learned about them below:

Jews

This was a moment of crisis for all who were present that day. Before Lazarus was raised from the dead there were basically two kinds of reaction from the Jews. Can you list what these two reactions were? (hint verses 36-37)

Reaction # 1 (vs. 36)

Reaction # 2 (vs. 37)

This is usually our two responses to tragedies: Those that say; "yes God does love me", then there are those that say; "God could have prevented this from happening if He had wanted to". Or we think that because God didn't do anything that He wasn't anywhere around when it happened. This only leaves us bewildered and confused and leaves us open to bitterness and feeling like God failed us. This is the response we find when Jesus comes. A hint of blame is heard as they tell Him that if He had come this wouldn't have happened. But in this moment of confusion; in this moment of great sorrow and conflicting opinions, Jesus has them do something that no one thought imaginable.

Read verse 39-41 and record what request Jesus made.

_____

_____

Can you imagine this scene even for a moment in your minds eye? How bizarre this must have been to the crowd that was watching that day.

How many days had Lazarus been dead when Jesus told them to remove the stone?

_____

The Jews of that day believed that the spirit or soul of a person hovered for three days over their dead body before leaving permanently. I believe Jesus waiting until the fourth day had significant meaning for the Jews. They would know without doubt that Jesus had the power to restore life where there was no life.

What was Martha's response to Jesus request?

_____

What was Martha's focus on?

_____

What had Martha just confessed that she believed about Jesus in verses 22-27?

_____

_____

_____

They had wrapped up the body of Lazarus after preparing him for burial and they laid him in a cave or a tomb as we know it and they rolled a stone over the mouth of that cave to seal his body in. That had been four days ago and now Jesus is telling them to roll the stone away and that if they believed they would see the glory of God! What a moment of faith that was standing before them. It's true, as Martha had said there would be a stench from any body that had been dead for four days. This was the reality of the situation. They knew Lazarus was dead because they had watched him die and they had prepared his body with the herbs and spices before carefully wrapping him in linens and placing him in the tomb. By this time, Lazarus' body would have already started to decay, he was probably unrecognizable at this point. But yet Jesus said, *"Remove the Stone"*.

Jesus told Martha that if she believed she would see the glory of God. This wasn't the first time Jesus had raised someone from the dead. There were two other times that Jesus raised others from the dead that were recorded for us in scripture. Look up these accounts and note what you learned from each.

- **Luke 8:41-56** (this same account is also told in Mark 5:35-42)

This is the story of a man named Jairus, an official from the Synagogue, whose daughter became sick and died. He comes to Jesus for help while his daughter is still alive. Read what happens and write down what you learn. Note any similarities or differences with this story and that of Lazarus.

_____

_____

_____

- **Luke 7:11-17**

This is the story of a widow woman whose only son had died. Note what you learn from reading this passage. Are there any similarities or differences in this story compared to that of Lazarus.

_____

_____

I think you would agree that even if we had never had any experience with the loss of a loved one or friend that we would say, just from reading these stories, that death brings grief to the heart of man. We have seen people weeping in all three of these accounts of someone dying. Death for most of us is hard to accept, difficult to bear. We have also come to know from this passage that people who are grieving need to have faith if they want to see the glory of God. Faith is vital to all of us but especially during times of grief.

What was different about these two events compared to Lazarus?

_____

_____

Although we don't know how long the son of the widow had been dead, we do know that during these times people were usually buried within 24 hours of death due to the rapid decomposition of the body. Remember these places are extremely hot and dry and they did not have the embalming capabilities that we do today, so burials happened rather quickly after one's death. So we can safely assume that the girl and the son had only been dead for a short time whereas Lazarus had been dead for four days.

It's interesting to note that Lazarus' name means: *"God has helped"*. How fitting this name became to Lazarus after Jesus raised him from the dead. But even more meaningful is that God looked ahead in time and named Lazarus or marked him out as the one whose life would be helped by the hand of God. Jesus had told the disciples that this will not end in death but will be for the glory of God. Jesus knew the ending, because he knew the beginning!! He was there when Lazarus was formed, for He was with the Father during creation. Jesus was there before Lazarus ever took his first breath for Jesus breathed life into him. Jesus was his life giver from the beginning and He would be in the end as well!

What did Jesus tell Martha in verse 25 of John Chapter 11?

"I am the _____ *and the* _____*; he Who believes in me will live even if he dies".*

We've already looked at it in verse 40, but it bears repeating: Jesus tells Martha very plainly that; "if you believe you will see the glory of God". If we believe Jesus said, we will see God's glory. Wow! The power of faith precious student, it is the power of faith.

PRINCIPLE

FAITH REVEALS THE GLORY OF GOD.

Jesus had told His disciples in Matthew 17:20; *"If you have faith as a mustard seed you can say to this mountain be ye removed and it will be moved".* Jesus never said it had to be a lot of faith! Aren't you glad for that? We have a difficult enough time with the mustard seed size faith and a mustard seed is so tiny!

The moment that Jesus told them to roll away the stone they had a choice to make. The first response was from Martha who didn't understand that Jesus was going to raise Lazarus from the dead. There was a hesitation at that moment. And then Jesus asked that heart-piercing question; "did I not say to you that if you believe you will see the glory of God?" It took incredible faith to roll that stone away. Faith will roll the stone away!

BENEFIT

OBSTACLES ARE REMOVED

Jesus was looking toward the greater glory. He was looking beyond the temporal and into eternity. You see Jesus knew what the outcome was going to be. He knew that ultimately in the end joy would be restored and God would be glorified in a way that He could not have if the circumstances had been different. The difficulty lies in whether or not we desire the greater glory and whether or not we believe God when He says that it will be for the greater glory. How often have we prayed to God, "I pray that you would get the glory"? But do we realize what we are really praying? God's glory could mean our suffering and many times it does. Moses prayed this prayer with great earnestness and desperation:

- Exodus 33:18

What was Moses' prayer to God in this verse?

_____

_____

What stones are there keeping you from life precious student?

_____

_____

152

In the original Greek when Jesus tells Lazarus to "come forth" literally it can read; "Lazarus this way out!". I love that! Jesus was calling to the one he loved showing him the way out from death. Lazarus was symbolic of the soon approaching death and resurrection of Jesus Himself. Jesus was the way to life. If Jesus had come sooner before Lazarus died then Lazarus could not have died! We never see anyone in scripture dying in the presence of Jesus; we only see them living! Why is this? Jesus told us Himself why this is true when He said; "I am the resurrection and the Life". Death cannot stay and it cannot come in the presence of Life!

What obstacles are in your life that hinder you from seeing the way out? Hindrances that are sealing you off from the master? Faith in the hands of God will roll these out of the way and He will show you how to get back to Him. Death is not to be feared or grieved over.

Review your memory verse and see if you can quote it to someone from memory. Thank you for being a faithful student of God's Word. The rewards are eternal precious one. I will see you on day four. Bye for now.

DAY FOUR

The following is a story from Missionary Warrior by Lettie Cowman.

A captain of a steamer, who was a devout Christian, recalls a life-changing encounter he had with one of his passengers. The ship was off the coast of Newfoundland and had encountered a dense fog. The captain had been on the bridge for twenty-four hours straight and had never left it. One of the male passengers came to the captain and said, "Captain, I have come to tell you that I must be in Quebec Saturday afternoon". "Impossible", the Captain replied. "Very well, if your ship cannot take me, God will find some other way. I have never broken an engagement for fifty-seven years. Let us go down into the chartroom and pray."

The captain looked at the man and thought to himself; what lunatic asylum can this man have come from? The captain had never heard of such a thing. He replied to the determined passenger; "do you know how dense this fog is?" "no," the man replied, "my eye is not on the density of the fog, but on the living God, who controls every circumstance of my life." The man then knelt down and prayed a very simple prayer. When he had finished the captain was going to pray also; but before he could, the man put his hand on the captain's shoulder and told him not to pray saying; "First, you do not believe He will answer, and second I believe He already has." The captain was astonished not to mention very humbled. The man looked deep into the captain's eyes as he went on to say; "Captain, I have known my Lord for fifty-seven years, and there has never been a single day that I have failed to get audience with the king. Get up, Captain and open the door, and you will find the fog gone." The captain did get up and found that indeed the fog was gone. On Saturday afternoon George Mueller was in Quebec for his engagement.

George Mueller was a man of great faith. We read about heroes of the faith such as him and others who had faith to move mountains and we seem to think; that could never be me! The reality of living the kind of life that George Mueller lived seems out of reach to most of us. I pray that our lesson time today will bring your heart hope in the matter of faith. Pray before you begin. Hebrews 11:6 tells us that, *"without faith, it is impossible to please God"*. During times of difficulty, tragedy, grief, pain, confusion, faith will be the one thing that will steady you. Our goal today as we finish this week's lesson is to see what true faith is and how it is exercised. We remember the words that Jesus spoke: *"If you believe, you will see the glory of God"*. This is our motivation today! To be women who believe and in the believing see God's glory.

Let's return once again to John Chapter 11. I want us to focus on Jesus' words in this passage. Take a highlighter and highlight everything that Jesus says in our verses of study. If you will look for the word "said" you will spot these easily. This will take a little time but it will be a powerful thing when you see it!

Once you've finished highlighting these places, see if you can fill in what Jesus says in each place provided. I've divided Jesus sayings into two parts: Jesus words before He arrived at Bethany and His words after He arrived at Bethany.

His Words before He arrived at Bethany

Vs 4, But when Jesus heard this, He said, "This sickness

_____

_____ "

Vs 7, Then after this He said to the disciples, "Let us_____

_____

_____ "

Vs 9, Jesus answered, "Are there not_____

_____

_____ "

Vs. 10, "But _____

_____ "

Vs. 11, "This He said, and after that He said to them,_____

_____

_____ "

Vs. 14, So Jesus then said to them plainly, "_____

_____ "

Vs. 15, "and I'm _____

_____
"

Before we go to part two of Jesus words let's look at this first half. Think with me a moment. Jesus was sent word of what?

Lord, behold, he whom you love is _____.

What did Jesus do when He received word that Lazarus had died. We know that Jesus knew that Lazarus had died because He tells his disciples this. So how did Jesus know that Lazarus was dead?

_____

Interesting question isn't it? In verse four Jesus tells His disciples that Lazarus sickness would not end in death, yet Lazarus does die. In verse 11 Jesus says, "I go, so that I may awaken him out of sleep." We know that Jesus was speaking of raising Lazarus from the dead because of what He says later in verse 14 that Lazarus was dead. Jesus had made His intentions very clear, He was going to Bethany to raise Lazarus from the dead.

Just from what Jesus has spoken thus far would you say that Jesus believed Lazarus would be raised? Explain your answer.

_____

_____

Jesus was pretty much committed at this point wasn't He? He had already purposed and committed to raising Lazarus from the dead. Jesus wanted His disciples to believe therefore He said to them, I'm glad I was not there, for your sakes.

Based on the words of Jesus so far, why do you think Jesus waited and did not go to Lazarus while he was still alive?

_____

_____

I believe that Jesus waited so that the disciple's faith would be increased. Jesus wanted them to have faith! He knew that His time on earth was drawing to a close and that His disciples would need to have faith especially after He was gone. This was His hearts desire, not just for His disciples but for Martha and Mary and the Jews that would be gathered there to witness it and for all of us who read this account. The Lord will use times of great difficulty to increase our faith.

Let's go through the second half of Jesus sayings, hold on it gets even better! Continue looking for the word said and highlighting any sayings of Jesus in the remainder of our passage and fill in the spaces below.

His Words After He Arrived at Bethany

Vs 23, Jesus said to her, "Your_____

_____"

Vs. 25, Jesus said to her, "I am_____

_____"

Vs 26, "and everyone who_____

_____"

Vs 34, "and said, "Where_____"

Vs 39, Jesus said, "Remove the_____."

Vs 40, Jesus aid to her, "Did I not say _____

_____?"

Vs 41, then Jesus raised His eyes, and said, "Father,_____

_____

_____."

Vs 42, "I knew that_____

_____

_____."

Vs. 43, When He had said these things, He cried out with a
loud voice,"_____."

Vs. 44, Jesus said to them, "Unbind him,_____

_____."

Did Jesus ever ask God to raise Lazarus from the dead?

_____

To Jesus the raising of Lazarus was no problem. The
chief difficulty was to remove the unbelief, the hesitancy
from Martha so that the glory of God would be revealed.
When Martha met His condition, which was the last step
of faith for her, Jesus took the next step. Jesus never
asked God to raise Lazarus, He thanked the Father for
having already answered! So great was Jesus faith in the

Father He assumed this task was as good as done. Jesus then addressed the dead man.

Look up John 5:24-28 and record what you learn about Jesus.

_____

_____

Look up the following verses and record what you learn about faith from each:

- Romans 1:17

_____

- Romans 14:23

_____

- Luke 17: 5-6

_____

- Mark 11:22-24

_____

- I Corinthians 2:5

_____

- Galatians 2:20

_____

- I Thessalonians 3:10

_____

- James 2:20

_____

- I John 5:4

_____

One more precious student!

- Hebrews 10:38-39

_____

Verse 39 talks of a faith to the "preserving of the soul". Turn to your Word Windows Section and look up the word Preserving and write out its meaning below.

Preserving (KJV-saving) _____
_____
_____
_____
_____

How marvelous it is when God peels away a layer, opens a window, and let's us see a whole new view! The kind of faith that the Hebrew writer was talking about was a faith of possession. This is a life changing truth, are you ready for this?

WE DON'T POSSESS FAITH, IT MUST POSSESS US.

This precious student is the secret to great faith. Great men of old, like George Mueller, Charles Cowman, and Hudson Taylor just to name a few, found this secret and lived by it. They discovered that we don't possess faith it possess us. Faith is not something that we get or that we have, but rather it must have us! This is the kind of faith that Jesus was talking about when He said to Martha; "if you believe, you will see the glory of God". In other words; if you allow faith to possess you, control you, you will see God glorified. This is why Jesus never had to ask out loud for God to raise Lazarus, He believed it to be so even when it wasn't so. He was controlled by His faith.

Do you remember what Jesus said when Lazarus came forth from the tomb bound in burial linens? He said, "unbind him and let him go". At that moment Lazarus resurrected life began. He was now a new person, for he had been raised to walk in newness of life. Jesus goal was not to remove the grief, but to restore life and in restoring life bring glory to God.

You may say; "Pam I prayed and I believed but still my loved one died". Yes it's true we can believe with all of our hearts that God is able and yet not get our prayers answered in the way we would like. This is where the value of knowing this faith truth comes in. If you are being controlled by faith then it won't matter what God does or doesn't do. It will only matter that God is glorified in it. The glory is always found in the resurrected life and that will be in eternity. God desires for us to live the resurrected life, meaning that life is a picture of His glory for the entire world to see, that they may believe in His Son, the Lord Jesus Christ. Grief will come into our lives as sure as the sun rises but we can know that God has already seen the outcome and will be there for the glorious ending.

What is the precious benefit of a faith that possesses us? It is that...

ℬENEFIT

RESURRECTED LIFE BEGINS

What happened to the spectators after they saw Lazarus raised from the dead?

_____

_____

It is only the resurrected life that can display the power and glory of God. The life that is dead cannot do this. This last miracle that Jesus performed was the one that would seal His own death and it's through His death that we can have the resurrected life. This is what Jesus was trying to show His followers. "I am the Resurrection and the life". It's all about Jesus.

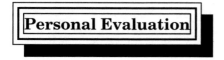

Personal Evaluation

Is your life a display of God's glory?

Are you trying to possess faith rather than allowing it to possess you?

What changes in your thinking and behavior do you think the Lord would want you to make as result of this lesson?

Week In Review

Principle	Benefit
Tragedies serve a higher purpose	Greater Glory Revealed
Jesus cares for Me	A place of Comfort is found
Faith reveals God's Glory	Obstacles are Removed
We don't possess faith, it possess us	Resurrected Life Begins

You are such a diligent student to have made it this far. Bless you precious student. I pray that you will hide this precious secret of faith in your hearts inner most chamber and allow it to control your life. It's a secret that most never discover in their lifetime. God has been very good to us to reveal it in His Word. Why don't you close this week's study out at the feet of Jesus pouring your heart out to the only one who can give you the resurrected life.

I will see you in our lesson time together. Much love to you my friend.....

May I invite you to have a seat at the feet of Jesus and may you linger there for a while.

NOTES

John 11: 1-45

1. Now a certain man was sick, Lazarus of Bethany, the village of Mary and her sister Martha.

2. it was the Mary who anointed the Lord with ointment, and wiped His feet with her hair, whose brother Lazarus was sick.

3. So the sisters sent word to Him, saying, "Lord, behold he whom You love is sick."

4. But when Jesus heard this, He said, "This sickness is not to end in death, but for the glory of God, so that the Son of God may be glorified by it."

5. Now Jesus loved Martha and her sister and Lazarus.

6. So when He heard that he was sick, He then stayed two days longer in the place where He was.

7. Then after this He said to the disciples, "Let us go to Judea again."

8. The disciples said to Him, "Rabbi, the Jews were just now seeking to stone you, and are You going there again?"

9. Jesus answered, "Are there not twelve hours in the day? If anyone walks in the day, he does not stumble, because he sees the light of this world.

10. But if anyone walks in the night, he stumbles, because the light is not in him."

11. This He said, and after that He said to them, "Our friend Lazarus has fallen asleep; but I go, so that I may awaken him out of sleep."

12. The disciples then said to Him, "Lord, if he has fallen asleep he will recover."

13. Now Jesus had spoken of his death, but they thought that he was speaking of literal sleep.

14. So Jesus then said to them plainly, Lazarus is dead.

15. And I am glad for our sakes that I was not there, so that you may believe; but let us go to him."

16. Therefore Thomas who is called Didymus, said to his fellow disciples, "let us also go, so that we may die with Him."

17. So when Jesus came, He found that he had already been in the tomb four days.

18. Now Bethany was near Jerusalem, about two mile off;

19. And many of the Jews had come to Martha and Mary, to console them concerning their brother.

20. Martha therefore, when she heard that Jesus was coming, went to meet Him, but Mary stayed at the house.

21. Martha then said to Jesus, "Lord, if you had been here, my brother would not have died.

22. Even now I know that whatever You ask of God, God will give you."

23. Jesus said to her, "Your brother will rise again."

24. Martha said to Him, "I know that he will rise again in the resurrection on the last day."

25. Jesus said to her, "I am the resurrection and the life; he who believes in Me will live even if he dies,

26. And everyone who lives and believes in Me will never die. Do you believe this?"

27. She said to Him, "Yes, Lord; I have believed that you are the Christ, the Son of God, even He who comes into the world."

28. When she had said this, she went away and called Mary her sister, saying secretly, "The Teacher is here and is calling for you."

29. And when she heard it, she got up quickly and was coming to Him.

30. Now Jesus had not yet come into the village, but was still in the place where Martha met Him.

31. Then the Jews who were with her in the house, and consoling her, when they saw that Mary got up quickly and went out, they followed her, supposing that she was going to the tomb to weep there.

32. Therefore, when Mary came where Jesus was, she saw Him, and fell at His feet, saying to Him, "Lord, if you had been here, my bother would not have died."

33. When Jesus therefore say here weeping, and the Jews who came with her also weeping, He was deeply moved in spirit and was troubled,

34. And said, "Where have you laid him? " They said to him, "Lord come and see".

35. Jesus wept.

36. So the Jews were saying, "See how He loved him!"

37. But some of them said, "Could not this man, who opened the eyes of the blind man, have kept this man also from dying?"

38. So Jesus, again being deeply moved within, came to the tomb. Now it was a cave, and a stone was lying against it.

39. Jesus, said, "Remove the stone," Martha, the sister of the deceased, said to Him, "Lord, by this time

there will be a stench, for he has been dead four days."

40. Jesus said to her, "Did I not say to you that if you believe, you will see the glory of God?"

41. So they removed the stone. Then Jesus raised His eyes, and said, "Father, thank You that You have heard Me.

42. I knew that You always hear me; but because of the people standing around I said it, so that they may believe that You sent Me."

43. When He had said these things, he cried out with a loud voice, "Lazarus, come forth."

44. The man who had died came forth, bound hand and foot with wrappings, and his face was wrapped around with a cloth. Jesus said to them, "Unbind him and let him go".

45. Therefore many of the Jews who came to Mary, and saw what He had done, believed in Him.

Forgiveness

Have you ever struggled with guilt from past sins? Most of us could and would answer yes to this question. Who hasn't done something at one time or another that we absolutely regret doing? Which one of us would not have at least one thing that if we had it to do all over again we would make a different choice than the one we did at the time. Why is this? It's called hindsight. Hindsight can be a curse and a blessing at times, for with hindsight comes the wisdom to make better choices in the present, but also with hindsight comes guilt often times robbing us of our peace in the present. We can be at perfect peace and all it takes is a subtle reminder of our past to bringing with it a flood of shame and regret. There's an old hymn that I learned as a child that says:

> *"Sin will keep you longer than you ever*
> *thought you'd stay*
> *And sin will cost you more than you ever*
> *thought you'd pay"*

How do we deal with past sins, past mistakes and live a life of joy and service to the Lord? How do we honor the Lord with our lives when we feel so unworthy at times, because of the choices we've made in the past? The first step is learning the truth of God's forgiveness. Jesus told His disciples; "You shall know the truth and the truth shall set you free". Well, precious student, we are going to learn the truth about forgiveness and in the learning be set free! We're going to study one of the most precious stories in the Word of God. We're going to look at the anointing of Jesus' feet. It's a heart touching story and one that will transform your thinking about forgiveness if you seek God's truth in the midst of it. Pray before you begin.

To help you understand the setting of our story: a man named Simon, who was a Pharisee, has invited Jesus into his home to dine with him. I'm sure the Pharisee had a lavish meal prepared for this "prophet" named Jesus. After all Jesus had been healing people of their diseases and He had just raised a young widow's son from the dead. Jesus was an important guest in that home on this particular evening. But as the meal is served and Jesus is reclining there something happens that will forever change the life of one woman. Let's look at it together shall we?

Our main text of study this week will be Luke 7: 36-50. Read through this account and then go through the passage again this time marking every reference to the woman who anointed the feet of Jesus by drawing a circle around her in the color of your choice.

Make a list of everything you learned about this woman by marking the text and list them in the box provided.

The Anointing Woman

This woman brought something with her; what was it?

_____

Why had this woman come to the Pharisee's home?

_____

_____

How did she approach Jesus?

_____

_____

Turn to your Word Window Section and look up the definition for **sinner** as seen in verse 37 and record it in the space provided.

Sinner _____

_____

_____

_____

Very little is told to us about this woman other than she lived in the city and heard that Jesus was dining in the home of this man Simon. Many have taken the view that she is Mary Magdalene of from whom Jesus cast out seven demons, but there is no scriptural support. The scriptures do tell us that she was a sinner. Based upon the meaning of this word, how would you describe the life of this woman? What picture do you get in your mind?

_____

_____

This woman has been my hero many times as I have read about her and thought about her over the years. I can't wait to meet her some day in glory and thank her for this act of love written down for me to read. This sinful woman, as the scriptures tell us, came to the place where she knew Jesus was. Because her hair was unbound gives strong opinion that she was probably a prostitute. She never says a word when she arrives to see Jesus and she comes from behind Him, showing her shame and guilt and her attitude of unworthiness to approach Jesus. She does the only thing that one in her condition could do; she falls at His feet and there weeping she pours out her heart. She begins lovingly pouring out the perfume she had brought with her and using her hair, she wipes and anoints His feet. She does not care who is there and she does not care who sees her. She never asked permission, she only silently begins her anointing. The only sound that is heard is the sound of weeping. What a sweet sound this must have been to the ears of Jesus. He never stops her, and He never condemns her because He knew that she was sorrowful of her sins. What a loving Savior we have precious student. He wants me and you to see His heart or He wouldn't have left this story written down for us to see.

Look up the following verses and note what you learn from each concerning God:

- Psalm 34:18

_____

- Psalm 51:17

_____

- Isaiah 66:2

_____

One more verse I want us to look at a little more in depth that is one of my favorite passages in the Bible. It's Isaiah 57:14-19 and it's typed out for you below. Once you've read through it, go back through it a second time but this time I want you to take a colored pencil and draw a triangle around every reference to God. The triangle symbol is so wonderful for God showing us that He is three in one. My personal color choice for God is purple, but feel free to choose your own! This passage needs time to soak into your heart so don't rush this exercise. The heart of God is so clearly seen in these verses and I don't want you to miss anything.

Isaiah 57:14-19

14. And it will be said, "Build up, build up, prepare the way, Remove every obstacle out of the way of My people."

15. For thus says the high and exalted One Who lives forever, whose name is Holy, "I dwell on a high and holy place, and also with the contrite and lowly of spirit in order to revive the spirit of the lowly and to revive the heart of the contrite.

16. "For I will not contend forever, nor will I always be angry; for the spirit would grow faint before Me, and the breath of those whom I have made.

17. "Because of the iniquity of his unjust gain I was angry and struck him; I hid my face and was angry, and he went on turning away, in the way of his heart.

18. I have seen his ways, but I will heal him; I will lead him and restore comfort to him and to his mourners,

19. Creating the praise of the lips; Peace, peace to him who is far and to him who is near." Says the Lord, "and I will heal him."

You can step back and look at this page and see all those beautiful triangles standing out before you! Do you know what that's doing? It's yelling from the page at us saying, "here I am, here I am". That's why marking key words in Bible study is so helpful to discovering truths.

Once you completed marking every reference to God, make a list of everything you learned about God and record it on the chart provided for you.

God

When you take the time to really study the heart and character of God it will leave you in awe and wonder.

Turn to your Word Windows Section and look up the definitions for contrite and humble. This will help you see a more beautiful picture.

Contrite _____

_____

_____

_____

Lowly (KJV-humble) _____

_____

_____

_____

From these word meanings, how would you describe a person who is contrite and lowly in spirit?

_____

_____

_____

From this passage in Isaiah, where does it say that God dwells?

_____

_____

This passage tells us why He dwells where He does. What reason does God give for this?

_____

_____

This sinful woman knew that she was a sinner and her heart's desire was for forgiveness. She was remorseful of her sin, she was crushed, and had been brought very low. When we see how she approached Jesus, we understand that she was a woman of a contrite heart, a woman of a lowly spirit. And praise to Jesus He did not turn her away! Nor will He turn you or me away when we come to Him in the same manner. We see here this beautiful principle.

PRINCIPLE

A CONTRITE HEART IS WHAT THE LORD DESIRES.

Aren't you glad precious student? When we approach the Lord with a contrite heart, a heart of humility, He will never turn us away! He loves us and wants us to come into His presence but not with pride or a flippant attitude regarding our sins. But rather He wants us to be remorseful and broken over our sins so He can accept us into His presence; because that's the place He wants us to be!

How have you approached God in times past?

_____

_____

What kind of heart does the Lord desire of you precious student?

_____

_____

It's when we are careless in our approach to God that God's heart is displeased. We should never become so comfortable that we forget we are unworthy to come into His presence. We should always come with a heart wanting to please and in full acknowledgement of our desperation for Him. I believe this woman was desperate for Jesus. Desperation for Jesus will always find welcome with Him. No wonder it was recorded in history in the Word of God, because it was such a rarity to see. And so it is even today. Very few are desperate for Jesus. We are desperate for more money, more friends, bigger cars, happiness, vacations, security, success, health and so on, but how many are truly desperate for Him?

Often times we hide our sins and are found to be prideful not wanting to come to God in humility. By nature we hate to admit when we are wrong, or when we have failed. No one wants to say of themselves, "I did it, and I have no one to blame but myself". When we come before the Lord with no excuses, no pleas because we recognize fully that we are unworthy of anything from Him then He opens wide His arms of love to us and says; come on in. He never, never turns away a contrite heart, NO NEVER. This principle brings with it this powerful benefit: Oh that you will never, ever forget it. When we come before him with a contrite heart we...

ℬENEFIT

WILL HAVE AN AUDIENCE WITH JESUS

There are thousands upon thousands of women who are so ridden with guilt from past sins that they don't believe the Lord would even allow them to come to Him in prayer, let alone forgive them. I've met many women through the years of ministry that have felt this way. Maybe you are one of these women who would say; "yes that's me". I understand, for I too am often overwhelmed with guilt from my past and at times, I've hesitated to even go into the Lord's presence because of it.

I understand! I have told the Lord many times, "Father I want you to know that I still grieve over my past sins". But do you want to know something dear friend, He has never turned me away! I have never lacked His attentive ear and love and acceptance when I come before Him in humility and with heart's desire to please Him and to be right with Him no matter the cost. We will look at how to deal with past sins that we have been forgiven of and the guilt that often comes with it later in this week's study, so worry not. I do want to ask you a few questions as we end our day together.

Personal Evaluation

- Where is your heart concerning sin?

- If your heart is humble before Him will He turn you away?

This sinful woman took a chance many might say. But I believe she made a choice, a choice to humble herself and throw herself upon the Mercy of Jesus Christ. She knew He would not cast her away for He had come to save her. She saw Him not just as a Savior but as her Savior, not just a Redeemer but her Redeemer, the One and Only who could forgive her of her sins. Where do you run precious one when you have sinned, when you have failed?

I pray that you will not only run to, but fall at the feet of Jesus in utter desperation and brokenness. And it's in this falling that you will find peace.

Our memory verse for this week is I John 1:9. Look it up and write it out below so you can begin memorizing it.

I John 1:9

I will see you on day two. Love and gratitude for you dear student.

I hope you are ready for another day friend. Pray before you begin!

Turn to our passage of study this week found in Luke 3:37:50 found at the end of this lesson. On day one we marked every reference to the sinful woman. Today I want us to mark every reference to Jesus using our symbol of a red cross. Don't forget to get all the pronouns as well.

Make a list of everything you learned about Jesus from marking this passage. Remember don't rush this exercise because this is where the fruit of inductive Bible study pays off. Truth can never be taken away from you so make sure you take the time not to miss it.

Jesus

Jesus' reaction to this situation astonishes me every time I read this story. Jesus had accepted the invitation from a Pharisee to come to a banquet in his home. The social customs of that day permitted needy people to visit such a banquet to receive some of the leftovers. Here He is in the home of a Pharisee eating dinner when all of a sudden a woman who obviously had a bad reputation came and began anointing His feet in front of everyone. She was not only anointing His feet, she was kissing His feet and weeping over them. In spite of this Jesus wasn't taken by surprise, and He certainly wasn't embarrassed of this woman in any way. I want us to look at Jesus in our time together today. He will be our focal point. What a wonderful focal point to have, amen?

From what you've gleaned from the scriptures so far, does Jesus react to this woman in any way?

_____

_____

I believe this event centers on two characters other than Jesus and that is the Pharisee and the sinful woman. The Lord wants us to see more than just a story about the anointing of His feet. Go through the text again, this time draw a box around every reference to Simon the Pharisee with a color of your choice.

Make a list of what you learn about the Pharisee from your markings.

Simon the Pharisee

What was the Pharisee's opinion of the woman and what she was doing?

_____

_____

What was the Pharisee's opinion of Jesus? (Look carefully and you will find it)

_____

_____

The Pharisee thought to himself that Jesus probably wasn't a prophet because if He were, He would have surely known what kind of woman it was that was touching Him. More than likely Simon probably invited Jesus to dine with him more out of curiosity than anything else. His thoughts reveal his opinion of Jesus; that little word "if" says a lot to us about this man's heart. Jesus' answer to Simon's unspoken objection (which constitutes the true heart of this story) proves Him to be a prophet indeed. Jesus saw the sin in Simon's heart and with prophetic authority says to him: "I have something to say to you". If the Lord said that to us we would listen right up wouldn't we? The Pharisee seemed more than ready to listen because he replies immediately, "say it, teacher".

Did the Pharisee ever address Jesus as Lord?

_____

Read through verses 41-42 and note what this "something" was that Jesus wanted to say to Simon the Pharisee. What was the story about?

_____

_____

What do you think Jesus was trying to teach Simon the Pharisee through the story He told?

_____

_____

Jesus had something he wanted to teach Simon and to all of us who read this account. Simon's attitude is typical in Christendom today, a self righteous, indignant heart! Simon wasn't concerned with his own sin, as Jesus points out to him, and he wasn't even concerned with Jesus. After all he thought he was a teacher and had his doubts if he were even a prophet. Jesus wanted to teach Simon something; the truth about his own heart. Simon need not be concerned with the woman, but with himself as we see Jesus so graciously point out. Let's compare what the woman did for Jesus and what Simon did not do for Jesus. You can find this very easily in verses 44-46.

Woman did for Jesus	Simon did not do for Jesus

When we look at this comparison would you say that the Pharisee was really concerned about Jesus? He had asked Jesus to dinner right? He even implied that Jesus did not need to let a sinful woman touch him. It would appear that maybe he had Jesus' best interest at heart. What do you think?

_____

_____

The story of the two debtors shows us that it doesn't matter how much debt you owe, a little or a lot, you must be forgiven just the same. Debt in this story is a picture of sin. We all have sinned no matter how much or how little and therefore we are all in need of forgiveness. Self-righteousness is exposed in the heart of this Pharisee because of the act of humility of this woman. Humility is a powerful tool in the hands of God to expose self-righteousness in the lives of others. Self-righteousness will always pour forth from a cold heart. This is what self-righteousness does to the heart of man, it not only blinds, but it hardens the heart. Just because the Pharisee invited Jesus into his home, and fed him a meal, did not mean that he loved or respected Jesus. It's not in what we do for Jesus, it's what we do **with** Jesus that matters the most. The message to this stony heart that night was the truth that everyone has sinned.

PRINCIPLE

ALL HAVE SINNED.

To help reinforce this truth precious student, let's look at a few verses. Record what you learn from each.

- Romans 3:23

_____

- Romans 3:9-12 (this is referring to Psalm 14)

_____

- I John 1:8

_____

- Proverbs 20:9

_____

- Romans 7:18

_____

- Isaiah 64:6

_____

_____

Once we grasp this truth that we are sinners in need of the Savior, and that nothing good dwells within us then we can come to Jesus. When we believe and understand that no one is righteous apart from Jesus and that we are all in need of forgiveness no matter how much we have sinned or how little we have sinned, then an amazing benefit comes flooding into our lives.

BENEFIT

SELF RIGHTEOUSNESS IS ADDRESSED

As we have seen from the Lord's comments to the Pharisee, he had not done anything for Jesus when He entered his home. He had not offered Jesus any water to wash His feet, let alone actually washed His feet for Him. He had not offered Him any affection as this woman had kissed His feet continually. He had not anointed His head with oil but this woman had anointed Him with costly perfume. In those times and even still today in many parts of the Middle East, the custom of anointing someone's head with oil when they entered your house was a sign of hospitality and a sign of honor to the one entering your home.

I want you to look up a couple of verses that will give you insight into the meaning of self-righteousness. Record what you learn beside each.

- Galatians 2:16

_____

_____

- Romans 10:1-4

_____

_____

Self-righteousness is just what it says it is: a righteousness that comes from self!

Jesus asked Simon in Luke 7: 44, "do you see (or seest, KJV) this woman?"

Turn to your Word Windows Section and look up the word see and record the definition in the space provided.

See (KJV-seest) _____

_____
_____
_____
_____

From your word study what do you think Jesus meant when he asked Simon if he could "see"?

_____

_____

Self-righteousness will never bring honor to Jesus and it will never show Him a heart of genuine love. Self-righteousness will never see its need for Jesus and it will always condemn. This is what Jesus wants us to see in this beautiful story. The self-righteous are never seen at the feet of Jesus! But the needy and lowly are found there.

It doesn't matter what you've done, or what your past involves, it matters only what He's done for you and how you respond to what He's done. We can fall at His feet and love Him for it or we can judge those who do and miss who Jesus is.

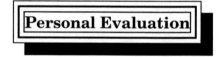

Personal Evaluation

Do you see yourself as a sinner?

_____

Do you recognize your need for Jesus or only the need that others have for Him?

_____

_____

A sign of self-righteousness is noticing what everyone else is doing wrong and not yourself. When we are busy looking at others faults we will most often miss our own! Well there is more to come beloved student. Look over your memory verse and I will see you on day three!

Welcome back precious student. I hope you are rested and are ready for another time of sitting at His feet together. Remember to pray before you begin asking the Lord to open your eyes that you may behold wonderful truths from His Word. It's going to be a great day as we study His Word together. As you remember, we've been studying the sinful woman who came and anointed the feet of Jesus while He was dining in the home of a Pharisee named Simon. Let's start our study today by reading through our passage of study this week found in Luke 7 that is typed out for you at the end of this week's lesson.

Write out verse 47 below in the space provided. I want us to look at how Jesus describes this woman's character.

Vs 47, "For this reason I say to you,

_____

_____ "

Did Jesus recognize that this woman was a sinner?

_____

How does Jesus describe her? He basically tells us three things about her personally, see if you can find what they are and list them below:

_____

_____

_____

Jesus said, that this woman had many sins, not just a few but many sins! It's important for us to know what sin is. We don't want our view of sin, or especially the world's view of sin, but we want to look at God's view of sin.

Look up the following verses about sin and record what you learn from each.

God's Definition of Sin

- I John 3:4

_____

- I John 5:17

_____

- James 4:17

_____

- James 2:9

_____

- John 16:9

_____

- Romans 14:23

_____

God is pretty clear about what sin is isn't He? All unrighteousness is sin. In other words anything that does not line up with God's Word is sin! This makes things real clear doesn't it? And for those things in our lives that the Bible may not clearly define, God goes on to say that if you know it's the wrong thing to do and you do it anyway, it's sin! If it's not of Faith its sin! God doesn't want any confusion or any excuses on our part. He wants us to understand clearly what sin is.

You may say, "well big deal, so I have sin in my life". "What I do is not that bad so what's the harm, right?" "A little sin never hurt anyone did it?" Or we think that as long as our sin doesn't affect anyone else it really doesn't matter because it's our personal choice.

Let's see what God's word says about the effects of sin. Look up the following verses and note what you learn from each.

The Effects of Sin

• James 1:15

_____

• I Corinthians 15:56

_____

• Romans 6:23

_____

• Psalm 51:3

_____

• Isaiah 59:2

_____

• Proverbs 14:34

_____

Let's look at just one more: II Corinthians 5:21. What did God do because of your sin?

_____

Sin is very costly isn't it? Sin causes a separation between us and God. It causes God not to hear our prayers. Sin is a reproach or disgrace to many people.

Sin brings guilt because it is ever before us. Sin has the price of death and it cost Jesus His life.

PRINCIPLE

SIN HAS A PRICE THAT MUST BE PAID.

God's word is very clear on the price tag of sin. Sin demands a payment and it will and must be paid. Sin is but for a season but it's a price will be paid for all eternity. I've seen many a life, including my own, pay a price far greater than ever anticipated. How about you?

What has sin cost you in the past?

_____

_____

_____

Was it more costly than you had anticipated?

_____

_____

Sin grieves the heart of God because no one understands the great price of sin as much as He does for it cost Him His son. The world's motto is: "Play now, Pay later". Sin has a price that must and will be paid. What is the benefit of this principle, of this truth you might ask?

BENEFIT

DEATH

I'm sure you must be saying: "Pam, death is not a benefit"! You're right beloved student it's not, but unfortunately according to God's word the only benefit that sin gives is death. It brings death to a person's life, it will bring death to your relationship with God, it will bring death to your peace, and it brought death to Jesus. Sin will cost you far more than you ever thought you'd pay. Oh do you see it precious student? The sinful woman saw it! This is why she fell at His feet. She knew her sins and she knew what they had cost her! You will not be remorseful over your sin until you have known and understood the cost of it.

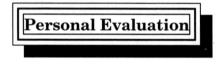

Personal Evaluation

Is there sin in your life that you have left unresolved?

Have you taken your sin lightly, thinking that it's really not hurting anyone or anything?

What would God want you to do concerning any sin in your life?

In closing I want to encourage you to take a look at sin through the eyes of God. God took and He takes sin very seriously. He took it all the way to Calvary. Will you? Why don't you fall on your knees before Him precious student and sit at His feet a while and listen.

I love you greatly. See you on day four.

DAY FOUR

Well this is our last day of this week together. I want us to look at forgiveness today and end our week with this freeing truth. Many people struggle with forgiveness and I pray that today God will show us truth concerning true forgiveness and set us free! Begin with prayer.

Let's read through what has been our passage of study this week found in Luke 7. Turn to the back and review the story so it will be fresh in your mind. Notice what the Lord says as he parts ways with this sinful woman. What were His last words to her? Write them out below.

Vs 48. Then He said to her

" _____ "

Oh to hear Jesus say those words audibly to us!! "Your sins have been forgiven". How this blessed woman must have rejoiced on the way out the door! Her life would be forever touched, forever changed, and forever free!! What a beautiful ending to this story. I want us to look at the depth of forgiveness that we have in Jesus. So we understand what forgiveness is, turn to your Word Windows section and look up the definition for forgiven that is used here in this passage and write it out below.

Forgiven _____

_____
_____
_____

Look up the following verses and record what you learn about forgiveness:

• Psalm 86:5

_____

196

- Luke 23:34

_____

- Psalm 130: 1-8

_____

_____

_____

- Jeremiah 31:34

_____

- Isaiah 38:17

_____

- Hebrews 10:17

_____

Just one more precious student!! It's one of my all time favorite verses concerning forgiveness. This verse will remove the guilt precious one if you will grab hold of it and believe God's Word for what it says.

- Psalm 103:12

_____

Whenever the waves of guilt flood over my soul and mind the Lord always brings this verse to my mind found here in Psalm 103:12, and when I remember this truth, waves of grace and mercy roll over me washing away all guilt! Jesus is so sweet like that to us when we are confronted with guilt. Guilt from sin that has been confessed and repented of is not from God. God's forgiveness is final therefore guilt is not associated with His forgiveness.

Would you be able to say with confidence that God wants and does forgive us of our sins when we come to Him humbly seeking His forgiveness? From the verses we just read the answer is clearly yes! God is a God that stands ready to forgive us of our sins.

Turn back to Luke Chapter 7 and look at verse 49. Once you've found it write it out below in the space provided for you.
Vs 49, those who were reclining at the table_____

_____

Where, is forgiveness found beloved?

_____

If you answered Jesus you are absolutely right. This is why Mary fell at the feet of Jesus and not the feet of the Pharisee! She looked only to Jesus, eyes fixed upon the one whom she believed to be her redeemer, her Savior. If she had not seen Jesus as redeemer she would not have fell at His feet in desperation. Oh this life giving truth that we so desperately need to cling to, and live by:

PRINCIPLE

FORGIVENESS IS FOUND IN JESUS CHRIST ALONE.

You cannot find forgiveness in works, in a pastor, in knowledge, in determination, not even within yourself. It cannot be found anywhere else beloved except at the feet

198

of Jesus. Let's look at a few verses together to help seal this truth for us.

- Daniel 9:9, where does forgiveness come from?

- Read Matthew 26:27-28; Jesus is about to go to Calvary and this is His last meal with His disciples. Note what He tells them about His blood.

- Hebrews 9:28; what did Christ bear for us?

- Hebrews 1:1-3; before Jesus sat down at the right hand of the father what do these verses tell us that he did concerning sin?

There is nowhere else to find forgiveness and no matter how great your deeds may be they can never earn forgiveness. Forgiveness is a free gift. I have shared God's Word with many who are working so diligently to earn God's forgiveness. God's Word teaches us that forgiveness is in Jesus and Jesus alone and forgiveness is never earned and it can never be repaid. I believe that's why this sinful woman anointed Jesus with perfume and wiped His feet with her hair to remove her tears. She understood that forgiveness is based solely upon the mercy found in the heart of God. This is why she cast herself low at His feet, she knew that forgiveness was a privilege that Jesus brought to her and she was fully aware that she was unworthy of it. Forgiveness is found only in Jesus and therefore...

𝕭ENEFIT

NO CONDEMNATION

Romans 8:1-2 is typed out below; read it precious student and shout it aloud!

Vs.1, Therefore there is now no condemnation for those who are in Christ Jesus.

Vs. 2, For the law of the Spirit of life in Christ Jesus has set you free from the law of sin and death.

God's forgiveness never condemns, therefore there is no longer any guilt! It's the song of the redeemed precious student, written with the blood of the Lamb of God. God has a heart to forgive us. He wants to forgive us or He never would have sent us Jesus.

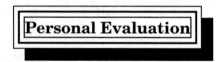

Have you been trying to earn forgiveness?

Do you believe that the only place to receive forgiveness is at the feet of Jesus?

Do you believe that Jesus will accept you into His presence no matter what you've done?

Week In Review

Principle	Benefit
A contrite heart is what the Lord desires	Will have an audience with Jesus
All have sinned	Self righteousness will be addressed
Sin has a price that must be paid	Death
Forgiveness is found in Jesus Christ alone	No condemnation

What a wonderful week we've had together. Thank you for giving your time to be at the feet of Jesus. How I pray that you will embrace God's forgiveness and know the life of no condemnation. Guilt will not stay where there is true forgiveness. Take a moment and review our memory verse for the week. I will see you in our teaching session!

Love you so very much.

May I invite you to have a seat at the feet of Jesus and may you linger there for a while.

NOTES

Luke 7:36-50

36. Now one of the Pharisees was requesting Him to
    dine with him, and He entered the Pharisee's house
    and reclined at the table.

37. And there was a woman in the city who was a
    sinner; and when she learned that He was reclining
    at the table in the Pharisee's house, she brought
    and alabaster vial of perfume.

38. And standing behind Him at His feet, weeping ,
    she began to wet His feet with her tears, and kept
    wiping them with the hair of her head, and kissing
    His feet and anointing them with the perfume.

39. Now when the Pharisee who had invited Him saw
    this, he said to himself, "If this man were a
    prophet He would know who and what sort of
    person this woman is who is touching Him, that
    she is a sinner."

40. And Jesus answered him, "Simon, I have something to say to you." And he replied, "Say it, Teacher."

41. A moneylender had two debtors: one owed five hundred denarii, and the other fifty.

42. "When they were unable to repay, he graciously forgave them both. So which of them will love him more?"

43. Simon answered and said, "I suppose the one whom he forgave more." And He said to him, "You have judged correctly."

44. Turning toward the woman, he said to Simon, "Do you see this woman? I entered your house; you gave Me no water for My feet, but she has wet My feet with her tears and wiped them with her hair.

45. "You gave Me no kiss; but she, since the time I came in, has not ceased to kiss My feet.

46. "You did not anoint My head with oil, but she anointed My feet with perfume.

47. "For this reason I say to you, her sins, which are many, have been forgiven, for she loved much' but he who is forgiven little, loves little."

48. Then He said to her, "Your sins have been forgiven".

49. Those who were reclining at the table with Him began to say to themselves, "Who is this man who even forgives sins?"

50. And He said to the woman, "Your faith has saved you; go in peace."

Healing Powers

DAY ONE

I had an uncle who was severely injured in a car accident when he was about 18 years of age. His body suffered brain, spinal, and other bone injuries. He lay in a coma for an extended period of time and the doctors gave very little hope to my grandmother for his recovery. My grandmother, a woman of great faith, had already buried one child and she did not intend on burying another one. She prayed fervently night and day beseeching God to heal her son and restore him to health. She called on many others to do the same and so, a prayer blanket was spread out over my uncle for many days. When there was no sign of healing, my grandmother called for men who claimed to have the gift of healing to come and pray over my uncle that he might be healed. She even had a famous evangelist come to pray and lay hands on her son but still her son was not healed.

Days turned into weeks and weeks turned into months and still my uncle lay in a coma with no sign of life and no sign of recovery. My grandmother continued steadfastly storming the gates of heaven through prayer, night and day refusing to settle for the answer of no! I believe God heard her cry and having pity on her, He reached down from heaven and touched the life of this18-year-old boy and woke him up out of his coma. He was not healed for he had suffered brain damage and other physical injuries that would leave him physically challenged for the remainder of his natural life. Although these were days filled with sadness, these were also days of great victory.

Bloodstains mark the pathway to heaven precious student and tears precede the harvester.

Why is there sickness and disease in our world today? Is there anything we can do in the midst of these challenges? What are we, as God's children, to do in the midst of sickness and suffering? There are those in Christendom today that believe if we had enough faith we would never be sick. There are teachings out there that go so far as to say, that it is not God's will for us to be sick. Needless to say, there is much controversy over healings, and sickness. It has divided many a church and many a religion. I believe we will see but one answer this week as we look at sicknesses and healings from God's perspective.

Although we'll be looking at several accounts this week, we will have one primary passage of study, so hang on, it will be well worth the effort! Pray before you begin beloved and ask God to help you approach His Word with openness and with a listening heart.

Turn to Mark 5:25-34 that is typed out for you at the end of this week's lesson and read through it one time to get the flow of the story.

In your own words what happens in this story? Who is involved...where does this event take place?

_____

_____

_____

Read through the story again but this time draw a circle around every reference to the woman in a color of your choice. Once you've finished, come back and make a list of everything you learned about the woman from marking the text. Take your time with this assignment and don't rush for there is much to see about this woman.

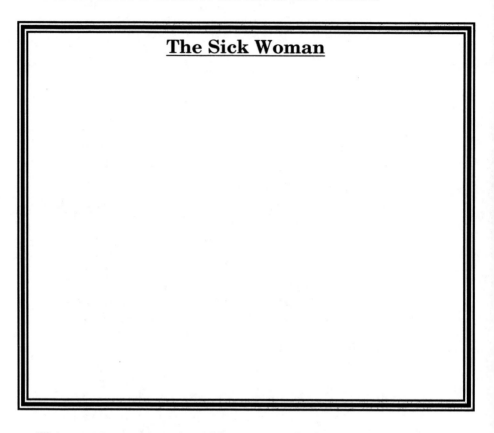

This same account is told to us in Luke Chapter 8:43-48 and Matthew 9:20-22. It's also typed out for you at the end of this weeks study. Read through these accounts and mark every reference to the woman the same way you did in Mark's account. Record anything new that you may have learned on your chart.

Would you say that this woman had done everything humanly possible to be healed of her sickness? What had she done to help her condition?

_____

Had her condition gotten better or worse?

_____

Exactly what sickness this woman had, the scriptures do not tell us. We do know that it was an issue of blood or a hemorrhaging of some kind that she had been suffering with for 12 years. This woman had exhausted all her energy, all her strength, all her resources, and yet her condition had not improved but only worsened with time.

Why did this woman come to Jesus? What does the scripture tell us that she was thinking?

_____

_____

_____

I'm so moved by the determination shown by this woman. She only wanted to touch His garments and even then only the hem of it. She did not want an audience with Him, she didn't even want to stop Him and interrupt Him even if it were only for a moment. She didn't want to ask or speak to Him, only to touch not even Him, but just His garments. It was not about a show for her, it was a quiet determination to get to Jesus. You see because this woman had an issue of blood she was considered in her day as one who is unclean. So in her thinking she knew she was unclean and therefore approached Him from behind and only wanted to touch His clothing and not Him. This woman is much like the sinful woman we studied earlier who knew she was unclean because of her sin, so she approached Jesus from behind.

Turn to your Word Windows Section and look up the word Touch as is used in Mark 5:28.

Touch _____

_____

_____

So this woman's intent at this moment in her life was to attach herself to Jesus, to lay hold of Him, to fasten herself to Him. To cling to Jesus! This was a woman with a purpose. Her hearts only desire was to grab hold of Jesus because she wanted to be made whole. She had nothing left at this point in her life. All of her money was gone, her health was gone, and she was weary from the years of suffering. But even in the midst of these, she pressed on to lay hold of Jesus. What truth do we see beginning to unfold before our eyes in this story?

PRINCIPLE

WE CAN COME EMPTY-HANDED TO JESUS.

What an awesome thing this woman did. The sinful woman if you remember came with perfume in her hands and she came to anoint Jesus. She came to give something to Him. But this woman who is sick comes totally empty-handed and in dire need. She had nothing to offer Jesus, nothing she could do for Him, for the state she was in would not have allowed her to. She comes only to receive! She came in full need of a Savior with nothing to offer Him in return. Oh the glory and beauty of Jesus that we see pour through this encounter. Let us look at a couple of verses together to help us understand what we are seeing in this powerful scene.

Look up the following verses and note what you learn about Jesus from each:

• Philippians 2:5-7

_____

_____

The word emptying in this passage can be translated to read: *"laid aside his privileges"*. With this meaning in mind, verse 7 could read: *"but laid aside His privileges, taking the form of a bondservant, and being made in the likeness of me."* In other words, Jesus laid Himself aside and all His privileges in order that He may become a bondservant of God. Jesus emptied Himself in order to fulfill God's purpose, which involved suffering. Laying aside ourselves, our privileges, is the challenge before us precious student!! This woman had to lay herself aside to do what she did.

- II Corinthians 8:9 (note what you learned about Jesus)

_____

_____

_____

_____

Let's look at one more passage that is found in Isaiah 53:1-10. It is typed out for you. Read through it once and then go back through it a second time marking every reference to Jesus by drawing a red cross. This passage is speaking of Jesus Christ and the life He lived here on the earth. Make a list of everything you learned about Jesus from marking these verses. These are powerful verses so take time to let the deep truths found here sink in to your heart and mind.

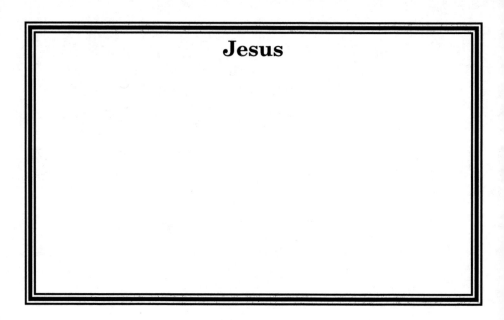

Isaiah 53:1-10

1 Who has believed our message? And to whom has the arm of the Lord been revealed?

2 For He grew up before Him like a tender shoot, and like a root out of parched ground; He has no stately form or majesty that we should look upon Him, nor appearance that we should be attracted to Him.

3 He was despised and forsaken of men, A man of sorrows and acquainted with grief; And like one from whom men hide their face He was despised, and we did not esteem Him.

4 Surely our grief's He Himself bore, And our sorrows He carried: Yet we ourselves esteemed Him stricken, Smitten of God, and afflicted.

5 But He was pierced through for our transgressions, He was crushed for our iniquities; The chastening for our well being fell upon Him, and by His scourging we are healed.

6 All of us like sheep have gone astray, each of us have turned to his own way; But the Lord has caused the iniquity of us all to fall on Him.

7 He was oppressed and He was afflicted, yet He did not open His mouth; Like a lamb that is led to slaughter, and like a sheep that is silent before its shearers, so He did not open His mouth.

8 By oppression and judgment He was taken away; And as for his generation, who considered that He was cut off out of the land of the living for the transgression of my people, to whom the stroke was due?

9 His grave was assigned with wicked men, yet He was with a rich man in His death, because He had done no violence nor was there any deceit in His mouth.

10 But the Lord was pleased to crush Him, putting Him to grief; if he would render Himself as a guilt offering, He will see His offspring, He will prolong His days, and the good pleasure of the Lord will prosper in His hand.

What was Jesus' attitude toward suffering?

_____

_____

Could you safely say that Jesus had emptied Himself or "laid aside His rights" in order to fulfill God's plan? Explain your answer.

_____

_____

Did Jesus know what it was like to suffer?

_____

Jesus understood what suffering was didn't He? He understood the life that had been completely emptied as a result of sufferings. Sufferings, beloved student, pour us out. Jesus embraced the sufferings that God had for Him, believing them to be part of His plan. Jesus saw sufferings through the eyes of the Father therefore He could accept them. I believe this woman knew and believed this about Jesus. She knew He would understand her need. Did you notice that this woman never asked Jesus to heal her? Her healing was not based on the asking, because she never asked! We are to come to God and make our request known, but what we see in this encounter is that asking wasn't necessary for her healing. She came absolutely needy; absolutely empty to the one she believed could give her what she needed. We can come empty handed to Jesus and...

ℬENEFIT

YOU WILL FIND WHAT YOU NEED IN HIM

Look in verse 34 of our passage of study in Mark 5. What does Jesus call this woman?

_____

This is the only time in the Gospels that Jesus addresses a woman by this word *"daughter"*. Daughter is such a personal term of endearment. In the Lord's eyes, she was His daughter because she came to Him believing He was the only one that could make her whole. As a child would run their earthly father so we are to run to the Lord. Oh daughter, you will find all that you need at the feet of Jesus for a child of the King will not be turned away.

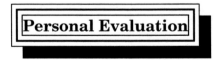

Personal Evaluation

What have you brought before Jesus in times past?

_____

_____

Have you ever come before Him completely emptied, having exhausted all your resources? If you can answer yes, write out a brief description of this time in your life and what happened as a result?

_____

_____

This woman had suffered for so long and yet her heart's desire was not to give up but to get to the healer. What is your greatest desire? Is it just to get to Jesus? Is it only to touch Him, not speak or make request, but just to touch Him. He will take you just as you are "daughter" and you will leave needing nothing, for needs fade away in His presence. He is greater than any need you have no matter how great. All He wants is you beloved.

I pray these truths will impact you this moment and will find you reaching, pressing to touch Him. May nothing or no one keep you from getting to Him.

I will see you on day two!

Welcome back daughter! I pray you are ready for another day sitting at the feet of Jesus. Pray before you begin.

Today let's jump right back in to where we left off yesterday! We have seen the life of this woman who has been sick for 12 years. She has seen many doctors and none have been able to heal her. She has spent all of her money and yet she had only gotten worse. When she comes to Jesus she has nothing to offer. She comes only to receive and then slip away quietly! But things didn't turn out that way for her did they? Let's look at our primary passage of study found in Mark 5:25-34. Read through it once just to refresh your memory. Take a moment and review everything you listed about this woman on your chart. Once you've finished go back through the text and mark every reference to Jesus by drawing a red cross. List everything you see about Jesus in this passage.

Jesus

_____

_____

Did Jesus realize that this woman had touched Him? If so, what did He do?

_____

These verses tell us that Jesus knew that power had gone out from His body. He knew that someone had received something from Him! Let's look at the word power that is used here. Turn to your Word Window Section and find the word Power and record it's definition below. The word "power" used in Mark is also the same word that is used in Luke and Matthew.

Power (KJV-virtue)_____

_____
_____
_____
_____

From what you've studied so far this week, how do you
think this woman felt towards her sufferings?

_____

I think we can safely say that she didn't want to be sick,
right? In fact I think most of us would answer the same if
we were in her situation. A sickness for twelve years
would take its toll on you. Let's look at some other
scriptures in God's Word that use this same word for
power: *"dunamis"*. Write out what you learned from each.
This is not exhaustive by any means but it will take you a
little time so hang in there with me. It will be worth it!

- Acts 1:8

_____

- Acts 6:8

_____

- Matthew 24:30

_____

- Romans 1:16

_____

- Romans 15:13 & 19

_____

- I Corinthians 1:18

- I Corinthians 2:4-5

- Ephesians 3:7 & 20

- Philippians 3:10

Almost finished...hang in there!

- II Timothy 1:7

- II Thessalonians 1:11

Whew! You did, I am so proud of you!! As we looked at these verses we saw that this same power that went out from Jesus is the same power that keeps us, saves us, works in us, reveals Jesus to us and much more!! This power is not just for healing but rather it is a complete power! Jesus said that He knew that power had went out from Him. Let's look at the woman's response when Jesus asked this question, which is found in verse 47 in Luke 8. Let me type out for you Luke 8:47 in the King James version. It was a blessing to me to read!

Luke 8:47

"And when the woman saw that she was not hid, she came trembling, and falling down before Him, she declared unto Him before all the people for what cause she had touched him and how she was healed immediately."

Finish this sentence: "the woman saw that she was
_____ _____."

The scriptures tell us that this woman was not hidden! She wanted her encounter with Him to be a private one. Capture this truth precious one: what happens in our private encounters will show in our public encounters. Powerful truth isn't it? When your life has been changed by the power of Jesus it cannot be hidden.

PRINCIPLE

A LIFE THAT HAS TOUCHED JESUS CANNOT BE HIDDEN.

When Jesus asked who touched Him, did this woman speak up on her own accord?

_____

Were others around to hear it?

_____

When you touch Jesus through prayer, through His Word, through drawing nigh to Him, He will touch others through you. This woman declared to all the people not only that she had touched the Lord, but she explained why she touched Him and what happened to her as a result of it. Praise flowed from her lips for all to hear.

Drawing near to Jesus will not only change your life but it will have the ability to change the lives of others who witness it. Testimony is a powerful tool that God uses. A life that has touched Jesus cannot be hidden because...

𝔅ENEFIT

JESUS' POWER IS REVEALED

What a challenging moment this woman was faced with. Can you imagine the scene with me?

> The streets are enthroned with people for Jesus had come to town. The crowds were unusually heavy and so this woman, being so sick, knew she must work diligently if she was to even get a glimpse of Jesus. After what seemed like hours she finally saw Him through the ocean of faces. But she was not satisfied just to see Him, she knew she must get to Him at all cost. She struggles through the crowd who were also trying to get to Jesus. All of a sudden she sees her chance. He is passing, coming near her direction. She was very weak by now, but pushing and struggling with every step she stretches out just barely able to touch the very hem of His garment as He was passing by. Her heart knew that she need only touch Him. Just a touch was all she needed! Immediately her life was restored! She could feel it and thankfully no one seemed to notice. But what was this? Jesus was stopping, He was turning around in her direction. He speaks a loud; *"who was it that touched me"*? At that moment she had a life changing decision to make, she could deny it and fade away into the crowd or, she could speak forth the truth. Everyone had stopped by this time; a hush had filled the streets for Jesus had asked a question. Everyone was looking for the one who had touched

Him. Though filled with fear she speaks out: "It's me, I touched Him! I touched Him that I might be healed and praise God I was!"

Though filled with fear, this woman's grateful heart gave in and she declared to all what Jesus had done for her. If we do not let others know that we have encountered Jesus, how will He ever get the glory from our lives?

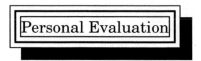

Personal Evaluation

Do you hesitate to speak the praises of Jesus? To speak of how He changed your life? If so, why?

_____

_____

Are you afraid to step forward and tell about Jesus saving power?

_____

_____

Do you long to touch Him, no matter what struggles stand in your way?

_____

What a powerful testimony this woman had. She was given the opportunity to share hers publicly for all to hear that day. Her life was changed that others might be changed. Like a *"city set on a hill"*, He cannot be hidden precious one. May you speak out about Jesus and say to all those who don't know Him: *"I have touched Him and He has made me whole"*. How pleased He will be with you daughter for this is what He asks of us: *"who is the one who touched me?*

Our memory verse for this week is:

II Corinthians 12:9

And He has said to me, "My grace is sufficient for you, for power is perfected in weakness."
Most gladly, therefore, I will rather boast about my weaknesses, so that the power of Christ may dwell in me.

Study this verse and I will see you on day three precious student. Thank you for your hard work today, I'm so proud of you. Hang in there with me and don't quit.

What a week we've had so far! We have seen a woman bound by sickness for many years, come to Jesus and immediately receive healing. We learned that her new life could not be hidden for Jesus demands for it to be confessed. I want us to continue with this powerful story as we look at sickness as seen in God's eyes. Pray first dear student and then begin.

Read the story to refresh your memory. We know from our study so far this week that this woman came for the sole purpose of healing, for she thought to herself; "if only I can touch His garments, I will get well". What purpose and strength this woman showed. Look at Mark 5:27 and write it out below.

Mark 5:27

_____

_____

What was her motivation to get to Jesus?

_____

Look up the following verses and note what you learn from each about sickness.

• James 5:10-13

_____

According to this verse in James, what is the one who is suffering to do?

_____

_____

- Romans 8:17-23

_____

_____

- II Corinthians 1:6

_____

- Hebrews 2:10

_____

- Hebrews 5:8

_____

- I Peter 4:1

_____

- I Peter 5:10

_____

One more verse precious student! Let's look at II Corinthians 12:7-10, which contains our memory verse for this week.
What purpose did these sufferings, these weaknesses, serve in Paul's life?

_____

Paul says that power was perfected through his weaknesses. Paul had a physical condition although we are not told exactly what it was, we know that he asked the Lord three times earnestly to remove it from him. God allowed it to remain so that He could teach Paul this wonderful truth. Sometimes God's greater glory is revealed by allowing the suffering to remain.

PRINCIPLE

WEAKNESSES WILL DRAW US TO JESUS.

Read Matthew 9:12 and note what it says about those who are sick.

_____

If this woman had not been sick, she would not have come to Jesus that day. Her sickness, her weakened condition, drew her to Him. Think about this truth with me. When do you come to the Lord in prayer the most? Isn't it when you are in a difficult situation? We tend to draw nearer to God in times of need more than in those times of ease and comfort-like reaching for medicine when you are sick, so God's heart is for us to reach for Him.

God will use the things that make us weak to make Him strong in our lives. Weaknesses are instruments in God's hands that will impart more of Him into our lives that we could not have gotten any other way. In these moments of weaknesses, when we draw near to Jesus...

BENEFIT

STRENGTH IS IMPARTED

How many times have you prayed: *"Lord make me strong"* or *"give me your power in my life"*? Do you realize what you are praying for? God's Word has clearly taught us that anything that makes us weak will make Him strong in our lives. God's power is imparted through weakness. This truth will give new eyes to sickness and suffering. So if God imparts something so wonderful, would God always want for us to be healed? Powerful question isn't it? Let me leave you with a few questions beloved student.

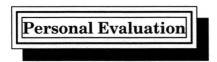

Personal Evaluation

Have you seen afflictions, sufferings, sicknesses, as a source of strength in your life?

Have you drawn near to Jesus to receive the power you need to overcome the weakness?

Do you desire the power of God in your life? If yes, then what might God use to give you that power?

Review your memory verse and I will see you on day four! Much love for you daughter.

DAY FOUR

It's been a wonderful, hard study so far this week and now we come to our last day together. Don't forget to pray precious student and then we'll begin.

Let's turn to the back of this week's lesson to Mark 5:25-34 and review our story. I want us to look at the last few verses today as this woman receives Jesus' parting words to her. Locate and write out below Mark 5:34.

Mark 5:34

And He said to her," _____

_____

_____
"

Jesus looked at the woman and told her that her faith had made her well. He also told her to go in peace and be healed of your afflictions. To understand the depth of what Jesus was telling her turn to your Word Windows Section and look up the definition for the following words.

Well (KJV-whole) _____
_____
_____
_____
_____

Faith _____
_____
_____
_____

In the light of these word meanings what do you think Jesus meant when He said to her, "thy faith has made you well (or whole)?"

The powerful thing we see about this word is that to be made whole may not necessarily refer to physical healing. It may not mean to deliver. It sometimes means to protect or preserve. I believe that there are times when God chooses not to heal but rather He chooses to preserve us in the midst of the suffering. Everything we could ever need or will ever need is found only in Him. We may not receive what we want when we run to Him, but we will always receive what we need! It's not always in the asking, for this woman never asked to be healed. It's not always in the amount of faith to receive healing but it will always rest with the Lord who wills and works according to His good pleasure. Because this woman relied on Jesus, she received power from His presence.

Let's look at a few places in scriptures of healings and note what we learn about them.

- Matthew 4:24

- Matthew 8:5-13

- Matthew 14:14

- John 4:46-53

- Acts 5:14-16

_____

Turn to your Word Window Section and look up the definition for sick as used in Matthew 4:24 and list its meaning.

Sick _____
_____
_____
_____

Now let's look at one more verse.

- James 5:14-16

_____

The word that James uses for sick is a different one the one that is used in Matthew. Turn to your Word Windows Section and locate the word sick as used in James 5:14.

Sick (vs14) _____
_____
_____
_____

In James 5:15 uses yet a different word for sick. See if you can locate this one in your Word Windows Section and write it in the space provided.

Sick (vs15) _____
_____
_____
_____

Why did James use two different words? We may not know for sure until we get to heaven beloved student, but I do believe he was trying to show us that sicknesses tire us and they make us weary. He encourages God's people to pray for those who are weak that they may be restored. Whatever James intended for us to know, we may not know in full, but I do believe that one thing we clearly see is that we are to look to God whether it be for healing or just for strength when we are weary from the sickness. God can absolutely heal any time He chooses, but He can also leave sickness and impart the strength we need to endure. Either way, God is glorified.

Jesus told the woman that her faith had made her whole. It came from Him but it was because she believed in Him. This was a powerful faith. This is a faith that means much more than just healing to us, it means restoration, for this woman was made whole. What a beautiful, beautiful truth.

Principle

FAITH RESTORES.

Faith does restore. In times when we are weary it can restore our strength. In times of discouragement it can renew our hope. Faith can and will weather the storms no matter how fierce. Faith will look disease, death, depression, and the very gates of hell in the face and cry with loudest refrain: *"My God will not fail me"*! This is the faith that restores precious one. Faith never disappoints. This is the moment where true power is found. It's not found in the healing but it's found in the One who can heal even if He chooses not to. Faith does restore and because it does...

ℬENEFIT

A LIFE OF PEACE IS FOUND

Jesus said to this woman "go in peace". Turn once more to your Word Windows Section and find the word meaning for peace and write it out.

Peace _____

_____

_____

_____

Beloved, we may not have all the answers we need or want but there is a place where we can find peace in the midst of it. This is true faith daughter. Casting yourself at the feet of Jesus not asking for anything, only wanting to be close, to touch Him. This is the only place we need to run. Peace is not something we reach out and hope to find; peace is what we receive when we place our trust or our faith in Jesus, for the outcome of every situation. We will see more about this faith in our lesson time together but for now we will call this our resting place.

In closing this week's lesson time together, I want to leave you with but one question. It's a question that you answer over and over again in different moments of your life.

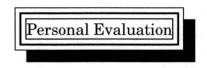

Personal Evaluation

Do you trust the Lord?

Let's take a quick review of this week's lesson

WEEK IN REVIEW

PRINCIPLE	BENEFIT
We can come empty handed to Jesus	You will find what you need in Him
The life that has touched Jesus cannot be hidden	Jesus' Power is Revealed
Weaknesses will draw us to Jesus	Strength Imparted
Faith restores	A Life of Peace is Found

How I have prayed for you precious student. Hang in there, we have one more week to go! How I pray that your eyes are beholding wonderful truths from His Word as you sit at His feet. Love to you.

May I invite you to have a seat at the feet of Jesus and may you linger there for a while.

NOTES

25. A woman who had had a hemorrhage for twelve years,

26. And had endured much at the hands of many physicians, and had spent all that she had and was not helped at all, but rather had grown worse.

27. After hearing about Jesus, she came up in the crowd behind Him and touched His cloak.

28. For she thought, "If I just touch His garments, I will get well."

29. Immediately the flow of her blood was dried up; and she felt in her body that she was healed of her affliction.

30. Immediately Jesus, perceiving in Himself that the power proceeding from His had gone forth, turned around in the crowd and said, "Who touched My garments?"

31. And His disciples said to Him, "You see the crowd pressing in on You, and You say, "Who touched Me?"

32. And He looked around to see the woman who had done this.

33. But the woman fearing and trembling, aware of what had happened to her, came and fell down before Him and told Him the whole truth.

34. And He said to her, "Daughter, your faith has made you well; go in peace and be healed of your affliction."

43. And a woman who had a hemorrhage for twelve years, and could not be healed by anyone,

44. Came up behind Him and touched the fringe of his cloak, and immediately her hemorrhage stopped.

45. And Jesus said, "Who is the one who touched Me?" And while they were all denying it, peter said, "Master, the people are crowding and pressing in on you."

46. But Jesus said, "Someone did touch Me, for I was aware that power had gone out of Me."

47. When the woman saw that she had not escaped notice, she came trembling and fell down before Him, and declared in the presence of all the people the reason why she had touched Him, and how she had been immediately healed.

48. And He said to her, "Daughter, your faith has made you well; go in peace."

Matthew 9:20-22

20. And a woman who had been suffering from a hemorrhage for twelve years, came up behind Him and touched the fringe of His cloak;

21. for she was saying to herself, "if I only touch His garment I will get well."

22. But Jesus turning and seeing her said, "Daughter, take courage; your faith has made you well." At once the woman was made well.

Worship At His Feet

DAY ONE

There is coming a day when all the tongues of men will sing with one mighty voice praises to the Lamb who was slain. They will cry out in sweet unity *"worthy, worthy, worthy, is the Lamb who was slain"*. On this day it will not matter what your social status was in life, it will not matter what the color of your skin is, how many friends you had, or how much wealth you had attained. On this day Jesus will be the only one that matters. On this day, the beginning of eternity as we will know it, every knee will bow before God's only son. He will come to take first place and all will acknowledge Him as Lord of heaven and earth. The old will pass away like a cloud and the new will rise as the morning sun. What a day beloved, glorious day that will be!

We were created for eternity; we were created to worship Him who sits upon the throne. Our study this week will take us into the heart of worship; it will take us to the feet of Jesus, for this is where true worship is! Amen? We will look from the first act of worship ever recorded in the word of God all the way to last act of worship. What a glorious week it's going to be for us as we journey to the depths of true heartfelt worship. Pray before you begin your study.

I want us to look in scripture at the very first place the word worship is mentioned in the Bible. It's found in Genesis 22:1-14. This is probably one of the most gut wrenching stories in the entire Bible. Abraham was 100 years old when Isaac, his son, was born to him and Sarah. He had waited so long for God to fulfill His promise to him that he would have a son, and from this son God was going to make a great nation. Then one day, Abraham's son was finally born. Can you imagine what the birth of that little boy meant to him? It was not only the blessings that having a child can bring to your life but also it was an added blessing to see God's Word come to pass before your very eyes. This birth was a very special birth because it was God's covenant with Abraham being honored. Then one day when the boy was still very young, God told Abraham to do something that was just unthinkable.

Let's read this story together. It is typed out for you at the end of this week's lesson.

Once you've read through a first time, go back through it again and see if you can find the place where worship is mentioned and put a circle around it of a bold color so it will stand out. This is the very first time that the word "worship" is used in scripture. Any time you come to a "first" mention of a word it often holds significant meaning as it usually sets a base rule for the use of that word through out the rest of scripture. They call this the "rule of first mention". So when studying a particular truth in God's Word it's always vital to go to the first place you see that specific word mention in scripture. It will usually be a foundational pillar for you in your study. The passage we will be studying gives us a beautiful picture of God providing Jesus for our sacrifice, but I believe the heart of this passage centers on worship. The deep truths that are here in this passage will change your life and the way you worship.

Turn in your Word Windows section and look up the Hebrew definition for worship that is used here in verse 5 of this passage. List the definition in the space provided.

Worship

_____

_____

_____

I want to give you a little more insight into the word worship itself: The English word worship comes from the Old English word **worthship**, a word which denotes the worthiness of the one receiving the special honor or devotion.

So when Abraham told the others that he and his son were going to worship what was he saying? Based on our word study of worship what do you think Abraham meant?

_____

_____

Let's go through our passage once more this time marking every reference to Abraham by drawing a box around him with a highlighter or colored pencil of your choice. Once you finished, make a list on the chart below of everything you learned about Abraham from your markings.

+---+
| **Abraham** |
| |
| |
| |
| |
| |
| |
| |
| . |
| |
| |
+---+

From what you've learned so far about Abraham, would you say that he had a heart for God? Explain why or why not.

_____

_____

_____

I want you to look closely at verses 4 & 5. Note what Abraham says as he raised his eyes and saw the place from a distance. What place was Abraham looking at? Verse five tells us. Write out what Abraham says and you will find the answer! I've started it for you.

Vs5 Abraham said to his young men, "stay here with the donkey, and _____

_____ "

Abraham refers to the place as "over there". What does Abraham tell his traveling companions that he and the lad are going to go do?

_____

_____

"Over there" was the place where Abraham was to worship God. What can you list about this place just from these two verses?

_____

_____

In case you didn't see it, these are the basic things that we see about this place. You may have seen something I didn't list, if you did that's wonderful!!

We see that this place:

- Was seen at a distance
- Abraham went to this place
- Abraham was to leave the others to go this place
- It was a designated place of worship
- It was a place he would leave at some point

Abraham was called by God to go and to worship at this place. So God called Abraham's heart toward worship of Him. God desires for us to worship Him. It's what He created us to do. Abraham saw the place of worship at a distance and then he said something life changing; "I and the lad will go over there". Here is our first principle for this week: I hope you're ready for this one:

PRINCIPLE

YOU CAN NOT WORSHIP GOD FROM A DISTANCE.

Why? Because, God never intended for us to watch worship from a distance but He intended for us to draw near to worship.

God calls us to engage in worship of Him. He never intended for us to see it with our eyes but rather to experience it in our hearts. What if Abraham had stopped and just sat down and been content to look at the place of worship from a distance? He never would have learned that God was Jehovah Jirah, *"The Lord Who Provides"*. He would have missed out on this incredible truth about

243

God. Because He drew near to worship God, Abraham experience God personally. God wasn't just a concept or a thought; He was very real and very personal to Abraham because Abraham wasn't content to watch the place of worship.

What did Abraham say after he said, *"I and the lad will go over there: and...*

You   finish   the   rest:
_____."

Abraham said that they would go over there and that they **would** worship. He was saying that if I draw near then worship will take place! Abraham's intentions were clear wouldn't you say? I love those words: *"we will worship"*. If only that were our determination! Every morning when we rise that we would say the same, "I will worship God". Have you ever seen anyone who was truly free to worship the Lord? Weren't they a blessing to watch? Many people envy others like this that are totally un-inhibited to worship God. When Abraham saw the place at a distance, he, at that moment, had a choice to make. When God reveals the true place of worship to us we are given the opportunity to go farther! Worship beckons the heart of God's chosen. It reveals itself at a distance that we may draw nigh.

Look in Genesis 22:2. How was Abraham to know the way to the place that God wanted Him to go to?

_____

God didn't want Abraham to just see the place of worship; He wanted him to journey there. Worship beloved student is a journey that will last our entire life. The wonderful thing about this is that God was going to lead the way for Abraham and so He will for us! God never gives a command without guidance!

244

ᴮENEFIT

GOD WILL LEAD THE WAY TO WORSHIP

God is a faithful guide precious student. He will never mislead us will He? We learned this truth in our first lesson together. When you sit at His feet you will never be misled.

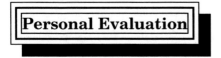

Have you worshiped the Lord, or have you only looked on at a distance never willing to journey there?

What keeps you from worshiping God freely?

What draws you to worship God?

Have you designated a "place of worship" in your home where you can bow and worship the Lord? A place away from the crowd, a place away from the noise?

Well this is the end of our session today dear friend. We are on our last week together. How I pray that you will learn and embrace the truths of Worship that we will see this week together as we sit at His feet. I will see you on day two. Thank you for a good day of study, how your Heavenly Father is pleased with you for this.

We've been studying this marvelous story of Abraham as he and his son journey together to worship the Lord God. It would prove to be the most difficult journey of his life, as we will see this week as we open up God's Word and sit at His feet. Take a moment and pray beloved.

Let's turn to our passage of study in Genesis that is typed out for you at the end of this week's lesson. Read through it once for a refresher and then let's dive in! If you remember from our study on day one this week, we marked every reference to Abraham and then made a list of what we learned about him from our markings. Today I want us to begin our study by marking every reference to God in our passage of study. In case you've forgotten our symbol for God it is a triangle. Mark every reference you see about God with a triangle as we've done before. Once you've finished, fill in the chart below with the things you learned about God from marking the text.

God

Let's look at a few verses and see what they say about worship. Look up each and record what you learn from each.

- Psalm 95:6-7

_____

- Psalm 99:9

_____

- Psalm 29:2

_____

- Revelation 14:7

_____

- Revelation 22:8-9

_____

Just as Abraham had been commanded to go and worship God on the mountain in the land of Moriah, so we are to worship God in the land of God's choosing. Worship is what God desires. Abraham knew that God wanted Him to worship Him and Abraham made a choice to obey God and true worship took place.

In Genesis 22:5, what does Abraham say to his young men?

_____

Abraham told his young men to stay while he and the lad went on ahead to worship. True worship comes from a heart of obedience. To worship God is to be obedient to what He has called us to do. We have all been called to worship Him. Worship should not be a choice for us but rather a natural response that flows from a heart of love and adoration for God who is above all. Abraham left the others in order to go and worship God. Which brings us to a powerful truth...

PRINCIPLE

WORSHIP IS THE ROAD LESS TRAVELED.

Abraham knew he must go this one alone and so he did. He left the others in order to worship God. A life of worship is often a lonely road because it is the road less traveled. Would you leave all others to worship the Lord? There are levels of private worship where you must travel to alone, for it is so very personal between you and God. It is at this level of worship that God is revealed. Abraham discovered God in a new way that day. He came to know Him as the God who will provide! Abraham would have missed this if he hadn't been willing to forsake all others and go to the place of worship. Our private worship with God will extend into our public worship of Him!   When we choose to travel that road less traveled...

BENEFIT

THE PLACE OF WORSHIP IS DISCOVERED

When you choose to leave the crowds and draw near to God you will discover that blessed place of worship that few ever find. This place of worship dear student will always find you at His feet. What a wonderful place to be found! We tend to think that worship is just a physical place such as a church or temple, but true worship is found in the heart of man when He is at the feet of Jesus. God intended for worship of Him to be a lifestyle for His children, not just something we partake in on Sundays. You were made to worship Him who sits enthroned above. The one who formed you with His hands and breathed life into you. The one who whispered your name the day you were born. How marvelous He is and worthy of all our praise and worship.

Our memory verse for this week is listed below. Take a few minutes to study it.

John 4:23-24

"But an hour is coming, and now is, when the true worshipers will worship the Father in spirit and truth; for such people the Father seeks to be His worshippers. God is spirit, and those who worship Him must worship in spirit and truth".

Personal Evaluation

Remember precious student that worship is a journey, one we travel every day of our lives. Every day bringing us closer and closer to the one who called us to worship.

How often do you separate yourselves from others that you may spend time with the Lord in true worship of Him?

Are you willing to travel the road less traveled if means great spiritual reward?

In closing I want to tell you that I love you and I have prayed for you that God will give you a heart of worship. If you don't have a heart of worship then pray and ask God to give you that heart that longs to worship Him. Place your heart in God's hands and ask Him to make it after His own. Why don't you steal away precious one right now and end our day together in a time of worship at the feet of Jesus.

I will see you on day three!

From the time that Jesus was born He was worshipped for He is worthy. Matthew 2:4 tells us that the wise men came and found baby Jesus and bowed and worshipped Him. We've been studying this encounter that Abraham had on a mountain that God had sent Him to. Let's dig in a little bit deeper today. Pray before you begin.

Let's begin today by reading through our passage of study for this week as found in Genesis 22:1-19. Once you've done that I want you to underline everything that God commands Abraham to do. It doesn't matter what color you use as long as it is a color that stands out from the rest of your markings.

Write out in the space provided everything that God commanded Abraham to do:

<u>God Told Abraham to:</u>

Do you think God was being unreasonable?

_____

What do you think God's purpose was in commanding
Abraham to do this?

_____

What kind of sacrifice was Abraham to make?

_____

Can you imagine being told by God to take your only son
and offer him as a burnt offering? *A burnt offering was
an offering where the whole offering was consumed by the
fire. Nothing was kept. The significance of the burnt
offering is that it represents the sacrifice of himself, soul
and body to God. It is the submission of his will to the
will of the Lord.*

Peloubet's Bible Dictionary

In view of the description of what a Burnt Offering is,
what do you think the scriptures mean when it tells us
that: *"God tested Abraham"* (as found in Genesis 22:1)?

_____

_____

What a beautiful picture we begin to glimpse of the
worship that God was calling Abraham to? This worship
would involve Abraham yielding his will to the will of
God. Not just in part, but in whole. It is a surrendering of
one's rights. True worship cannot take place unless one of
the parties involved surrenders their rights. This is what
Abraham had to do. Would he be willing to go all the way
with God no matter the cost? Would he surrender even it
meant his son's life?

Read verses 6-12 of our passage of study. Describe in your own words what Abraham does to carry out the will of God.

Abraham's actions of worship

Abraham went prepared to worship. He brought the wood, he had the fire, and he had the knife. But where was the sacrifice? Who had the sacrifice? Isaac even looked at his father and ask him where the sacrifice was that they were to offer. Isaac knew that you could not worship God unless you had a sacrifice!!!

Turn to your Word Windows Section and look up the word "offer" as used in verse 2. This is what the LORD told Abraham to do with his son Isaac.

Offer _____

_____

_____

_____

From this word meaning, we begin to get just a glimpse into what God was commanding Abraham to do. God told him to "offer up" your only son. God also let Abraham know that He knew and understood that he loved his son.

God knew what the cost was for Abraham. By asking Abraham to "offer up" Isaac, God was calling Abraham to a higher place of worship. We see this in the meaning of the word offer that is used in this verse. It was a journey for Abraham, a costly pilgrimage.

What was the cost of worship for Abraham?

_____

Had Abraham been in this position before or was this a new place for him?

_____

The worship that God was demanding of Abraham was one of total surrender and it was a worship that was costly. This brings us to our principle today.

PRINCIPLE

WORSHIP CANNOT TAKE PLACE WITHOUT SACRIFICE.

Why is this beloved? It's because worship is costly. Worship is sacrificial in action. This truth doesn't make us want to rush out and worship does it! In fact, most of us would say that the price for worship is too costly. Abraham made the choice to pay the price. Why? How could he have made such a choice? As a mother of two, I could not imagine paying such a price. I've asked myself many times, would I have said; "yes Lord, here I am". I believe that Abraham had completely surrendered himself into the hands of God. When we have surrendered, when we have offered ourselves as a burnt offering unto the Lord, then the cost is no longer our focus. Cost will not be an issue when we have surrendered.

Write our verse 8 of our passage of study.

Genesis 22:8

Abraham said, "_____

_____

_____ "

Do you see precious student? The cost of the sacrifice was not a concern to Abraham! Why...because, he had put his full trust into the hands of God. The cost of the sacrifice was in God's hands not Abraham. There were two times that Abraham *"raised his eyes"*, the first was to see the place of worship at a distant. What was the second thing that Abraham saw when he *"raised his eyes"*? See if you can find the answer and write it out below.

Abraham raised his eyes and saw...

_____

Abraham knew that worship was costly but Abraham also knew the benefit of paying the price of worship. Worship is costly but...

BENEFIT

WE WILL RECEIVE

Abraham saw a ram caught in the thicket! If Abraham would have been content to see the place of worship only he would have missed seeing the place of provision! Abraham went from seeing to receiving! God is the God who provides for us that we may worship Him. How awesome this is precious student! Worship is costly, but it is God who pays the ultimate price for worship! We are the ones who receive. When we obey God and offer ourselves completely unto worship we will find that the cost is nothing compared to the benefits we receive. We must be willing to look beyond our present circumstances if we are ever going to experience true worship.

Look at Genesis 22:15-18 and underline every benefit that Abraham received as a result of worship. Mark these in a color that you have not used in this passage before. Once you've finished, list these rewards out below.

The Rewards of Worship

In case you missed any let me give you the list of blessings

- Will be greatly blessed
- Will be greatly multiplied
- Will have victory over your enemies
- All nations will be blessed

Wow! Do you see this precious student? The rewards of worship far out weigh the cost! Worship is worth it wouldn't you say! God rewards the worshipper beloved. He always rewards the worshipper. If you are not a true worshiper, look what you are missing!

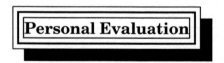

Personal Evaluation

Have you come to the place in your life where you have offered yourself up to God wholly and unreservedly?

Do you trust your God?
Is He worthy of any price?

These are sobering questions aren't they? Difficult, but necessary, I believe. This is why most never make the pilgrimage to worship God, because the cost is too great. They are not willing to give their time, their energy, or their affections and neither are they willing to leave their place of comfort. We must leave the common ground dear student, forsaking all others, paying any price, trusting completely no matter where He leads if we are to worship Him. All of creation is crying out in worship of its creator yet God's people are not. God is calling us to a higher place. He is calling us to worship.

I believe with all of my heart that God is calling His people to come back to the very heart of worship. He is calling us as a "burnt offering" to be laid upon the altar of worship. How many people attend church week in and week out never having truly worshipped God? The sad truth is that true worship is a rarity today. How many of us go about our every day lives and never take the time to bow before the Lord and worship Him privately as is pleasing to Him?

In closing out our time together today, write out your memory verse in the box below. See how much of it you can write out without looking!

Memory Verse (John 4:23)

Thank you for diligent study of God's Word. You are loved and appreciated so very much. I have prayed for you.

See you on day four!

Well we have come to our final day together precious student. We have been looking at the heart of worship this week and we want to bring this truth home in our time together today. We have seen so far that worship is a journey and it is costly. We know that worship is God's command of us and it is a choice of obedience. Let's begin today, our final day on our knees together at the feet of Jesus asking Him to do a deep work within us that only He can do. Ask Him to make your heart into a heart that beats as one with His. A heart that worships at His feet. I will pause now, even as I am writing this to pray for you, to go before you to the throne on your behalf, to the feet of my Savior. So know precious student when you reach this place, that someone has prayed for you.

Look up the following verses and write out what you learn about the people who will worship the Lord.

- Psalm 22:27-29

_____

- Psalm 66:4

_____

- Revelation 4:10-11

_____

During this study we have looked at Mary and Martha several times. I want us to close out this study looking at Mary, the sister of Martha and Lazarus. We have seen her sitting at the feet of Jesus, listening to His Word. We have seen her fallen in absolute grief at the feet of Jesus seeking consolation. Now I want us to look at a time when she was at the feet of Jesus in sheer worship and adoration. Turn to the end of today's lesson and find there John 12:1-8. Read this passage through and let it soak in. We have looked at the sinful woman who came to anoint Jesus seeking forgiveness, but here Mary is anointing Jesus in worship. Lazarus has just been raised from the dead and Jesus is eating a meal with them and His disciples. The Passover is at hand and so this is a very special time. It would be one of the last moments that these dear followers would have with the Lord on the earth.

Once you've read through this passage go through and mark every reference to Mary by drawing a circle over them in a color of your choice. Record what you learned about Mary from marking the text.

Mary

Here in this account, do we see that Mary received anything from Jesus?

_____

The other women, including Mary that we have seen at the feet of Jesus thus far have all come in need. They have all been on the receiving end. The first time Mary was at His feet, she was receiving His spoken Word. The second time we see her at His feet she is receiving comfort. The sick woman received healing. The sinful woman received forgiveness. The demonic man received freedom and Peter received salvation. But this account is different from all the others for there is no receiving of the one who is at the feet of Jesus. This is an act that is totally unselfish. It is the true heart of worship.

What did Mary give Jesus? What did it cost her to do what she did?

_____

Your memory verse is typed out for you below. What does this verse tell us about true worshipers?

_____

They worship in spirit and in truth. Can you imagine this scene with me. Here is a dinner that has been prepared for Jesus and His disciples. Sitting at the table was Lazarus who had just been raised from the dead! Once a dead man, four days in the tomb, was now reclining at the table eating dinner with Jesus. This resurrected man's sisters were present also. One sister was serving the dinner and the other was at the feet of Jesus anointing His feet with perfume. What a scene this must have been! The scriptures tell us that many people came to this place that night not to see Jesus only, but that they might see Lazarus as well. In the midst of this crowd, Mary worships Jesus. She is not in a Church, she is not in a private setting, in fact; she is in a very public setting.

261

But this is the moment that she chooses to worship Jesus by pouring out a very costly bottle of perfume. I believe there are times for private worship but there are times of public displays of worship! If you worship Him privately you will have no problem worshipping Him publicly.

What happens when Mary pours out the perfume and anoints Jesus? What happens to the place where she was?

_____

Did Mary's worship of Jesus have any effect on her surroundings, on others?

_____

Look up the following verse and mark every reference to "aroma" or "fragrance" note by drawing a box around each with a color of your choice. Record what you learned by marking the text.

II Corinthians 2:14-17

14 But thanks be to God, who always leads us in triumph in Christ, and manifest through us the sweet aroma of the knowledge of Him in every place.

15 For we are a fragrance of Christ to God among those who are being saved and among those who are perishing.

16 To the one an aroma from death to death, to the other an aroma from life to life. And who is adequate for these things?

17 For we are not like many, peddling the Word of God, but as from sincerity, but as from God, we speak in Christ in the sight of God.

What two types of aromas were there? (hint: vs.16)

_____

One aroma was from death to death and one was from life to life. The writer (Paul) goes on to tell us what this means. He describes two types of people in verse 15. List what these are in the space provided.

_____

Paul was saying that their lives were a fragrance of Christ to those who were lost, and to those who were being saved. Did everyone who witnessed what Mary did understand it? Did they all agree with it?

_____

Worship will not be received by everyone beloved student. There are those who will be saved through the aroma of it and there are those who will not. But the potential power of worship is seen. Our worship has an affect on others.

In these passages, how does the "fragrant aroma" affect others?

_____

When Mary anointed the feet of Jesus the room was filled with the fragrance. When true worship takes place it cannot be hidden. Mary came to give worship to the Lord. She came to pour it out. Our Principle for today is:

PRINCIPLE

WORSHIP IS TO BE POURED OUT ON THE LORD.

Worship was never meant to be given in moderation, but rather it is to be poured out lavishly upon the Lord. Mary was pouring out her worship at the feet of Jesus. What a beautiful aroma worship is as it ascends to the throne above. It is sweet in the Father's eyes and acceptable to Him. Mary saw Jesus as the One who was worthy of her worship. Jesus was not someone just to serve, to enjoy, or to run to in time of need, but He was the One to Whom worship was due. True worship comes from a heart of love for the object of worship. You will not pour forth worship upon someone whom you do not love. Worship is motivated by love. Jesus worshiped the Father in this same way.

Look at Ephesians 5:2 and note what you learn about Jesus.

_____

What keeps us from this kind of worship?

_____

Look up the following verses and note what you learned from each about worship and what hinders true worship from taking place.

- Isaiah 2:8

_____

- Matthew 15:1-9

_____

_____

_____

One of the keys to true worship is recognizing why we don't worship. Identifying the things that have kept us from worship? Worship is more than words spoken from our lips. True worship takes place when we worship in spirit and in truth. It never tells us that true worship takes place with words alone! Worship is an act of the soul based on what you know to be true about the Lord.

When true worship takes place; when it is poured out…

ℬENEFIT

THE EARTH IS FILLED WITH THE KNOWLEDGE OF HIM

Isn't this the highest form of worship beloved student? To fill the earth with the knowledge of Jesus. This is that aroma that offers life. The aroma the permeates every place it is poured out. Worship is contagious! He is worthy, worthy is the Lamb Who was slain!!. There is coming that day of worship where all will gather on the hills of glory and the streets of heaven will be filled with the fragrance of Jesus for we will pour out our lavish worship upon Him for all eternity!

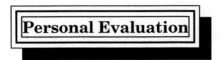

Personal Evaluation

Will you pour forth your worship at the feet of Jesus?

What is the object of your highest affection?

Is your life a fragrant aroma that fills the lives of others?

What would God want you to do right now as a result of this study?

Let's take one final look at what we have learned this week beloved student.

Week In Review

Principle	Benefit
You cannot Worship God at a distance	God will lead the way to Worship
Worship is the road less traveled	The place of Worship is found
Worship is costly	We will receive
Worship is to be poured out	The earth is filled with the knowledge of Him

Can you say your memory verse without looking? If not review it some more until you can recite it from memory. If you remember when we started this course you were asked to answer a few questions in a pre-journey assignment. I want to close today but taking you back to that assignment. What did you list there? What was your deepest desire to see God do in your life? Why do you think He has not done this for you? Do these sound familiar precious one.

Would you answer those questions differently now? Where can every answer be found? Where can you take every desire of your heart? Where can you run when you don't understand? Where can you run in times of need? Where can you run for deliverance? Where can you run for comfort when your heart is breaking? Where can you run precious daughter when you are suffering, when your life needs to be made whole? Where can you run when you need forgiveness? Where can you run for salvation?

The only answer you need ever know is:

At the feet of Jesus

Can you hear the voice of Heaven oh daughter?

> *The Spirit and the bride say, "Come". And let the one who hears say, "Come." And let the one who is thirsty come; and let the one who wishes take the water of life without cost.*
>
> Revelation 22:17

Every answer can be found in Him... every need met at His feet. May you be found at the feet of the One who gave His life for you that you may be free, that you may be whole. I pray that running to the feet of Jesus will become like air to you; you cannot make it one moment with out it. Thank you for taking this pilgrimage with me. I pray your life will never be the same. May you love Jesus with your life.

Love and Maranatha to you beloved...

May you not be found by the World, for you have been lost at the feet of Jesus.

NOTES

Genesis 22:1-14

1. Now it came about after these things, that God tested Abraham, and said to him, "Abraham!" And he said, "Here I am".

2. He said, "Take now your son, your only son, whom you love, Isaac, and go to the land of Moriah, and offer him there as a burnt offering on one of the mountains of which I will tell you."

3. So Abraham rose early in the morning and saddled his donkey, and took two of his young men with him and Isaac his son; and he split wood for the burnt offering, and arose and went to the place of which God had told him.

4. On the third day Abraham raised his eyes and saw the place from a distance.

5. Abraham said to his young men, "Stay here with the donkey, and I and the lad will go over there; and we will worship and return to you."

6. Abraham took the wood of the burnt offering and laid it on Isaac his son, and he took in his hand the fire and the knife, so the two of them walked on together.

7. Isaac spoke to Abraham his father and said, "My father!" and he said, "Here I am, my son." And he said, "Behold the fire and the wood, but where is the lamb for the burnt offering?"

8. Abraham said, "God will provide for Himself the lamb for the burnt offering, my son." So the two of them walked on together.

9. Then they came to the place of which God had told him; and Abraham built the altar there and arranged the wood, and bound his son Isaac and laid him on the altar, on top of the wood.

10. Abraham stretched out his hand and took the knife to slay his son.

11. But the angel of the lord called to him from heaven and said, "Abraham, Abraham!" And he said, "Here I am."

12. He said, "Do not stretch out you hand against the lad, and do nothing to him; for not I know that you fear God, since you have not withheld your son, your only son, from Me."

13. Then Abraham raised his eyes and looked, and behold behind him a ram caught in the thicket by his horns; and Abraham went and took the ram and offered him up for a burnt offering in the place of his son.

14. Abraham called the name of that place "The Lord will provide", as it is said to this day, "In the mount of the Lord it will be provided."

1. Jesus, therefore, six days before the Passover, came to Bethany where Lazarus was, whom Jesus had raised from the dead.

2. So they made Him a supper there, and Martha was serving; but Lazarus was one of those reclining at the table with Him.

3. Mary then took a pound of very costly perfume of pure nard, and anointed the feet of Jesus and wiped His feet with her hair; and the house was filled with the fragrance of the perfume.

4. But Judas Iscariot, one of His disciples, who was intending to betray Him, said,

5. Why was this perfume not sold for three hundred denarii and given to the poor people?

6. Now he said this, not because he was concerned about the poor, but because he was a thief, and as he had the moneybox, he used to pilfer what was put into it.

7. Therefore Jesus said, "Let her alone, so that she may keep it for the day of My burial.

8. For you always have the poor with you, but you do not always have me."

Word Window Section

Sitting (KJV-sat) *parakathizomai*
(is in the aorist tense) To sit down near, to sit down
beside. It expresses a simple action, usually indicates an
action prior to this event showing that there was a cause
for the action.

Listening (KJV-heard) *akouo*
(is in the imperfect tense) which means it is a continuous
action. It means to give audience to, a hearing to
understand.

Distracted (KJV-cumbered) *perispao*
to draw around or away, distract. It's used in the passive
voice, which gives us the picture of one who is over-
occupied. It gives us a picture of someone being drawn
around something or someone by other things. Things
that change our direction.

Worried (KJV-careful) *merimnao*
It means to be anxious about, to have a distracting care,
to take thought.

Bothered (KJV-troubled) *turbazo*
 To disturb or crowd.

Seeing (KJV-saw) *eid*
 It means to know by perception, to be aware of or to have
knowledge of, to be sure or to understand. It is a perfect
tense with a present meaning, signifying primarily, "to
have seen or perceived", "to know or have knowledge of".
It suggests fullness of knowledge, not just a progression of
knowledge.

Possess *daimonizomai*
Meaning to be exercised by a demon; possessed with
devils, or with the devil. vexed with a devil. It comes from

the root the word *daio;* meaning to distribute fortunes; a demon or supernatural spirit of a bad nature.

Imploring (KJV-besought) *parakaleo*
To call near, i.e. invite, invoke (by imploration, or consolation). It means to beseech, comfort, exhort, desire, and entreat. The most frequent word with this meaning, lit. Denotes "to call to one's side", hence, "to call to one's aid". It is used for every kind of calling to a person, which is meant to produce a particular effect, hence, with various meanings, such as comfort, exhort, desire, and call for.

Sickness *astheneia*
Feebleness, frailty, infirmities, lit. It means lacking strength, weaknesses, disease and sickness.

Deeply (KJV-groaned) *embrimaomai*
Intensive, it means strength, it primarily means to snort like a horse, to express indignation. To be painfully moved. It implies anger.

Troubled *torasso*
Meaning to stir or to agitate. It was a word used to describe a sea in a storm.

Wept *edakrusen*
It means to shed tears quietly.

Comfort (KJV-comforteth) *parakaleo*
It means to call near, invite, invoke by imploration, or consolation. It means to beseech, exhort, it's most frequent meaning is *"to call to one's side"* or *"to call to ones aid."*

Glory *doxa*
Primarily signifies an opinion, estimate and hence, the honor resulting from a good opinion. Doxa always

denotes a good opinion, praise, honor, glory, an appearance commanding respect, magnificence, excellence, manifestation of glory.

Believed pisteuo
To have faith in, upon, or in respect to, a person or thing. To entrust oneself to, be committed to one's trust. It means not just to believe, but also to be persuaded of; and hence to place confidence in. It signifies reliance upon.

Master epistates
an appointee over, used here for teacher.

Lord *kurios*
Supreme in authority, controller, one to who service is due.

Left (KJV-forsook) *aphiemi*
It means to leave, yield up, to let go, to give up a thing to a person, to depart from one and leave him to himself so that all mutual claims are abandoned. To go away leaving something behind.

Followed *akoloutheo*
To be in the same with. To reach. To be a companion of, expressing likeness and union with the one you are companions with.

Preserving (KJV-saving) *peripoiesi*
It means acquisition, purchased possession, to obtain.

Sinner *hamartolos*
sinful, can be translated immoral

Contrite *dakka*
crushed, lit. powder. To collapse or break. To crouch, it means to dash into pieces.

Lowly (KJV-humble) *shaphal*
depressed, low, lower, or base.

See (KJV-seest) *blepo*
It means primarily to have sight to see, observe, discern or perceive.   It indicates a greater vividness than just seeing, it expresses a more intent, earnest contemplation.

Forgiven *aphiemi*
It means to send away, to give up, to keep no longer, and to leave behind.

Touch *haptomai*
It means to attach oneself to. This word comes from the root word *"hapto"* which primarily means, "to fasten to". To cling to, or to lay hold of.

Power (KJV-virtue) *dunamis*
Comes from a root word meaning; force. It means mighty works, abundance, and miraculous power. Most always, this word points to new higher forces that have entered and are working in this lower world of ours. The effect being part for the course.

Well (KJV-whole) *sozo*
This word means to save, to deliver or protect. It also means to preserve, do well and to be whole.

Faith *pistis*
This word means persuasion, moral conviction. It means truth or truthfulness. It means a reliance upon. This word is used to describe the character of one who can be relied on. It is used of confidence.

Sick *(as used in Matthew 4:24)=kakos*
It means grievously sore, or to be diseased. It is used in the physical sense and in the moral sense. It denotes badly ill.

Sick *(as used in James 5:14) astheneo*
To be feeble, or to be weak. It means to be sick or diseased. It means weak or to be made weak. To be without strength or powerless.

Sick *(as used in James 5:15) kamno*
This word means to toil or to tire. To faint, to be wearied or sick. This word primarily signifies to work; then, as the effect of continued labor, to be weary

Peace *eirene*
Implies prosperity. It means: one, to join, or quietness. It describes a harmonious relationship with others, between nations or between man and God. It means freedom but not just from anxiety, but it means wholeness or completeness of life that come from being brought into a right relationship with God.

Worship *shachah*
The root word means to depress or to prostrate in homage to royalty or to God. It portrays the act of bowing down, to stoop or crouch. It means to fall down in reverence.

Offer *alah*
This word is used in a variety of senses. It means to go up, to ascend. It suggests movement from a lower place to a higher place. This word can mean to make a journey. It can mean, extend or reach. This word became a technical term for: "making a pilgrimage".

W.O.W. International, Inc.

W.O.W. International, Inc. was formed in August of 2005. Founder and President Pam Jenkins was led by God to form a ministry that focused on women receiving the Word of God. W.O.W. International, Inc. purpose is to reach and impact women around the globe with the Word of God, empowering and equipping them to be holy women of influence to the world they live in. Also to challenge women to be and do all that God has purposed through thought provoking Bible studies and Bible materials, radio and television programs, study tours, conferences, discipleship, counseling services, and the ministry of intercessory prayer.

W.O.W. International is a transdenominational ministry dedicated to Bible Literacy. It is our belief that God has gifted women with a unique power of influence. If you impact and influence women, you impact and influence the World. To that end, W.O.W. International seeks to reach every woman, every where, in every language with the message of the Cross of Calvary, with the message of Jesus Christ, that He is the Way, He is the Truth, and He is the Life.

If you wish to find out more about ministry opportunities offered by W.O.W. International, Inc. or about the author and other works, please write to us at:
W.O.W. International, Inc.
P.O. Box 849
McDonough, GA 30253
Or call us at (678) 232-5830.
You can also reach us at our website:

http://home.bellsouth.net/P/PWP-WOW2005.

There are teaching tapes that accompany each study. For those tapes or other W.O.W. materials, please contact us at the above listings.